HR How-To

Strategy

Everything you need to be strategic in your HR decisions ...

CCH Editorial Staff

Essential HR Solutions

A WoltersKluwer Company

Publisher: Catherine Wolfe

Editorial Director: Jeanne Statts

Portfolio Managing Editor: Mike Bacidore

Contributing Editors: Jan Gerstein, J.D.
                        Joy Waltemath, J.D.

Production Coordinator: Tina Roselle

Cover Design: Craig Arritola, Laila Gaidulis

Interior Design: Laila Gaidulis

Layout: Publications Design

This publication is designed to provide accurate and authoritative information in regard to the subject matter covered. It is sold with the understanding that the publisher is not engaged in rendering legal, accounting, or other professional service. If legal advice or other expert assistance is required, the services of a competent professional person should be sought.

ISBN 0-8080-1035-2
©2003 **CCH** Incorporated
4025 W. Peterson Ave.
Chicago, IL 60646-6085
1 800 248 3248
hr.cch.com

A WoltersKluwer Company

All Rights Reserved
Printed in the United States of America

Acknowledgements

CCH INCORPORATED gratefully thanks the following persons for their generous assistance with this project:

Jim Faletti, President
Strategic Insights, Ltd.
Lansing, IL

Brent Longnecker, CCP, CBP, President
Longnecker & Associates
Houston, TX

Paul Gibson, J.D., SPHR
V.P. Human Resources
CCH INCORPORATED
Riverwoods, IL

Colleen Plant, Senior Compensation Analyst
CCH INCORPORATED
Riverwoods, IL

Lynn Harshbarger, Senior Human Resources Generalist
CCH INCORPORATED
Riverwoods, IL

Editorial staff
Lisa Franke, CCP, SPHR
Joyce Gentry, J.D.
Jan Gerstein, J.D.
Theresa Houck
Lisa A. Milam-Perez, J.D.
Barbara Moore, J.D.
Lori Rosen, J.D.
David Stephanides, J.D.
Joy Waltemath, J.D.

Graphic designers
Laila Gaidulis
Craig Arritola

Production Specialist
Tina Roselle

Contents

What does it mean to be strategic?

Jorge is the newly hired HR manager for a manufacturing organization—one that until his position was created did not consider a need for an HR professional separate from general management. Jorge has entered a culture that has little experience with or respect for "just" an HR manager, yet Jorge is committed to making a difference. Where should he begin?

You can find hundreds of books, seminars, white papers, consultants and articles that address strategic human resources (HR). You can participate in roundtables and talk with your peers. You can search the Internet and search the library. Yet despite all this information and discussion, we often still are left with one question: What exactly does it mean for HR to be strategic?

This is a fundamental question, and it's fundamental to the entire profession of HR. In fact, HR spends a lot of time *talking* about it, but doesn't spend as much time *being* strategic. So let's answer the question.

How can HR be strategic?

Being strategic in HR means identifying the organization's business goals and the people capabilities HR needs to achieve those goals. It means understanding the company's strategic objectives and aligning HR's strategy to help meet those objectives. It means getting the right people with the right skills in the right place for the right price. It means asking HR's customers—top management, line managers and employees—where they're headed and how HR can help them get there.

DON'T miss this

HR is strategic. The people function of any organization is a strategic component of its business success. The problem is not that HR isn't strategic, it is that the people of HR don't act strategically.

Jim Faletti, President, Strategic Insights

Most people don't realize how much HR can help a business. HR professionals who are knowledgeable and flexible and who can use creative thinking skills can do a tremendous amount to help a company. HR is all about creative thinking—thinking of ways to anticipate problems, develop possible solutions as well as alternatives, save money, enhance productivity, enhance morale and otherwise manage the human capital that will help the business.

The term "human capital" typically means the knowledge, skills and abilities employees possess that enable them to function effectively in their jobs. How these resources are shaped and focused greatly impacts a company's success.

HR professionals are in a unique position because they are viewed as the internal expert and advisor on employment compliance matters as well as management concepts. As an HR professional, therefore, you are ideally positioned to understand how to align HR and the company's strategic objectives. This is in contrast to other types of managers, such as in accounting, marketing or production, who usually are focused solely on their functional responsibilities rather than how to get employees throughout the company to optimally perform their jobs.

Strategic HR takes a long-term, "big picture" approach to HR, according to Dr. John Sullivan, noted HR author, speaker and professor at San Francisco State University. He describes strategic HR as operating HR programs or initiatives with the goal of making a direct contribution toward meeting major corporate long-term objectives.

Rather than focusing on internal HR issues, a strategic focus means addressing and solving business problems through the effective use of people management programs. The primary goal of strategic HR is to increase employee productivity and corporate revenue.

What is or is not strategic is determined by senior managers outside of HR. They judge strategic actions or programs not by the words that describe them, but instead by their actual impact on business results, which incidentally, is always measured in dollars!

Dr. John Sullivan

Focus on the business first

Every business, no matter what it is, can be viewed as a three-legged stool. The top of the stool is a business plan and strategy. The legs of the stool are the tools necessary for propping up the business strategy: capital, technology and people. To behave strategically for the organization, HR needs to realize that the people aspect is one-third of the picture, no matter what. The stool—that is, the business strategy—falls down without it.

Start by focusing on the business plan that is the driving force of the organization. Then consider the third leg—the people leg—that helps to sustain it. Ask what you can do, with your functional expertise, to strengthen the "people" aspect of the business. Is it staffing? Is it employee relations? Is it benefits?

DON'T miss this

The key to strategic behavior is in how you approach your functional role: think first of the larger organization and its overall success; you are a business person and HR is merely your specialty.

HR professionals have thought of themselves for far too long as a unique function within an organization, distinct from the running of the business in the same way that operations, sales, and finance are, for example. However, HR is no more unique than any of these other functional areas; they all exist to serve the business plan and strategy.

What's the difference between being tactical and being strategic?

Compensation, staffing, performance management, policy administration and all other essentials of HR are not strategic. But neither are finance, accounts payable, operations or legal "strategic" in that sense. These are just the necessary elements in how you deliver on a strategy.

Strategic activities are very different from tactical activities, Sullivan explains. Tactical initiatives are programs, products or functions that have a major impact on reaching departmental or functional goals. Examples of departmental or functional goals include increasing attendance to the company picnic or participating in interviews with job candidates and asking good questions.

Tactical activities usually affect short- to medium-term goals. Activities are internally focused on the day-to-day functions of the HR department. Changes that are made generally are incremental, maintaining the status quo with minor adjustments as needed. In addition, tactical HR is typically reactive, responding as problems arise rather than anticipating situations.

In contrast, strategic initiatives make a major contribution toward helping the entire company meet its long-term objectives. Typically, metrics are used, and tools are provided to help employee productivity. Also, initiatives are prioritized by high priority business units or high priority company objectives. Examples of strategic business objectives include improving customer service, reducing costs or increasing market share.

> **Examples:**
> **Tactical training:** *Offering the same classes each year because they're well-attended and measuring how many people attend.*
> **Strategic training:** *Adding new training programs that create a measurable difference in on-the-job performance after an employee takes the class.*
> **Tactical recruiting:** *Cutting hiring costs by using cheaper but lower-quality Internet sources, bringing in new hires that perform below average or take longer to get up to speed.*
> **Strategic recruiting:** *Using metrics to identify the best sources for improving on-the-job performance of new hires.*

Focus on your strengths

As an HR professional, are you a "get in the trenches" type of person who wants to get involved, or a behind-the-desk "idea person" who wants to share them with your colleagues? Either way, you can be a contributor to the strategic direction of the company.

In order to be the most effective, you must know how your corporate culture works and what kind of people your top management relies on and trusts. Then modify the strengths of your work style with the preferences of your key leaders to accomplish your goals.

The industry in which you work can influence which approach to take. An HR professional in a nonprofit environment would need to be different from one in, for example, a healthcare organization. Cultures can be changed given enough time and support, but change is dificult for everyone. Not working within a company's culture can be a disaster.

Common elements of strategic HR programs

Now that you know what it means to be strategic, the next step is to put that definition into perspective so you can understand what actions you must take to move from being solely tactical to being strategic.

Being strategic starts with behavior on the part of the HR professional that says "I'm here for the good of the business, to make the business successful"—however "success" is defined at that particular point in time. That identification with and attachment to the business' success is the first step in behaving strategically.

When an HR department is strategically focused in support of business objectives, it typically manifests common characteristics and goals, and you can use these in developing your own strategic approach. According to Sullivan, these common elements include the following:

HR increases employee productivity and profits. HR provides programs and services that result in a measurable increase in employee productivity, revenue and return on investment (ROI). It builds a strong business case outlining its dollar impact and other intangible benefits.

HR has an external focus. HR ensures that its programs and staff focus their efforts on the problems and opportunities of the business rather than on internal HR issues. HR measures its success by its impact on business results.

An external focus assures HR efforts are aligned with business goals and with changes in the business environment. HR distributes its budget and time so that the highest percentages of resources are committed to programs that impact the organization's high priority strategic goals. HR prioritizes customers and activities based on corporate objectives.

HR helps build a performance culture. HR coordinates all of the company's resources to build a "performance culture" throughout the organization. HR drives this performance culture by ensuring that all managers, management systems, measures and rewards work together.

HR provides a competitive advantage. HR continually compares its programs to the HR programs at the company's competitors and provides programs superior to the competition.

HR makes fact-based decisions using metrics. HR continually measures the business impact of HR programs. It uses metrics to proactively identify potential problems and opportunities and to continually improve. Most people management decisions are based on facts and data, rather than opinions.

HR is proactive and future-focused. HR anticipates changes in the organization's business environment and adapts quickly as the business environment changes. HR seeks out business problems and opportunities and aggressively provides solutions. HR creates, rather than facilitates, change.

HR coordinates its efforts within the department. HR ensures that its programs and staff coordinate their efforts within HR to achieve results, speed, consistency and the highest customer satisfaction.

HR takes a global approach. HR ensures that programs have a business impact both locally and around the world.

HR builds a brand. Strategic HR is not satisfied with just "running good programs." HR must build a "great place to work" brand both internally and externally. Building a strong image gives HR stable funding, and it raises its business contribution by increasing retention and providing a steady flow of talented recruits.

Technology permeates everything. HR uses technology creatively and appropriately for metrics, paperless HR, 24/7 employee and manager self-service and globalization.

How HR impacts the bottom line

The key to impacting the company's bottom line is to align HR strategic activities with the company's strategic objectives so that HR can help achieve the company's objectives in a way that will positively affect productivity, revenue and profits.

Your organization's strategic direction

That means you need to know what the company's strategic plan is and what the objectives are, and those can be identified in different ways. Sometimes the CEO sets the major corporate objectives. Often, the strategic plan documents the company's goals. Even CEO bonus compensation factors reflect what the organization considers strategic.

If you don't have access to any of this information yet, ask for it. Management most likely will at least provide a copy of the strategic plan. Study carefully and consider where HR can provide support. Ask appropriate questions that demonstrate your understanding of the overall direction. Begin a dialog with other managers and senior leadership. If you're unsure of your business acumen, find a mentor.

Even if you're not sure of what your company's goals are or can't get access to the strategic plan, every company has similar long-term objectives that you can use to begin building your HR strategy. Sullivan notes that typical corporate goals can include:

- Building a competitive advantage into a product or service.
- Increasing revenues or profit.
- Cutting costs.
- Increasing market share.
- Improving customer service or product quality.
- Reducing product development time-to-market.
- Increasing employee productivity.
- Increasing shareholder value (stock price).

HR's complementary roles

A strategic HR department has several roles: strategic HR, administrative services, change agent and employee champion. Accordingly, an HR strategic plan should set deliverables, or goals, for each role in alignment with a business outcome, as follows:

Strategic HR. Align HR practices with business strategy by determining the leadership, skills, competencies, organization structure, rewards and development programs needed to execute the strategy.

Administrative services. Determine the right HR organization structure to cost-effectively deliver basic HR services, transactions and record keeping. Reduce HR costs, but deliver better service. Push the technology envelope.

Change agent. Create and facilitate a process that ensures line managers can close gaps in culture and workforce skills needed to achieve the strategy.

Employee champion. Provide employees with resources needed to meet increased demands and achieve corporate growth.

✓ ✓ ✓ **Checklist**

How to facilitate strategic change

Ask yourself these questions to help ease the process of making changes to fill strategic gaps:

- ☐ Who is leading the change?
- ☐ Do employees understand the need for change?
- ☐ Do employees understand what they'll do differently as a result of the change?
- ☐ Does HR recognize the system's implications?
- ☐ Is there a method to measure change?
- ☐ How do we keep attention focused on change?

Example: A finance company has the strategic corporate objective of establishing a customer relationship management process. HR creates a strategy with these goals to help achieve that objective:

- ☐ Develop an assessment profile to identify key qualities and skills to aid in the hiring process.
- ☐ Determine the reward and compensation structure necessary to hire and retain the best customer management employees.
- ☐ Develop job descriptions for this new position.

Examples of areas in which HR's tactical responsibilities can impact the bottom line can include:

- ◆ Recruiting and relocation expenses;
- ◆ Turnover and retention;
- ◆ Compensation;
- ◆ Health benefits;
- ◆ Retirement benefits;
- ◆ Training;
- ◆ Workers' compensation;
- ◆ Safety.

Examples: *At one organization, HR's safety and workers' compensation responsibilities become strategically aligned with the business goals when HR develops a business plan to improve production floor safety. HR justifies the investment, not only because avoiding accidents is the "right thing to do," but also because it understands the financial implications that, at a 5 percent profit margin, $100,000 in new sales is required to pay for a $5,000 accident. Increased profits result from lower accident costs.*

In any area in which HR is going to make a positive bottom-line impact, the HR professional must know and understand relevant state and federal laws, be knowledgeable about administration requirements, and most importantly, develop a relationship of trust with employees so they know that HR is working in their best interests.

Bottom-line focus is not enough

A common misconception among HR professionals who are attempting to get their arms around becoming more strategic is that they must focus solely on the bottom line, that every policy, procedure or directive, for example, must show a cost-justification that benefits the bottom line. While a bottom-line focus is an important aspect of business strategy and is an excellent tool, it may not be enough, because it's too compartmentalized. Instead, every policy, procedure and directive should be *business-success* focused.

The key is to focus on the overall success of the business and to add value to that every day.

Example: *Jorge felt he could make a difference in his new job at the manufacturing company by developing a strategic plan for continuous improvement. He felt that continuous improvement would provide a useful tool for employee development that would ensure short-term improvements in productivity and long-term improvements in profitability. So, he developed a business case with these goals:*

◆ *Implement a management development plan.*
◆ *Develop and implement a training program for production employees.*
◆ *Create a management scorecard that identifies high-, medium- and low-potential employees.*
◆ *Develop metrics around the efficacy of the training, retention and development of high-potential employees.*
◆ *Use metrics for the continuous improvement process that include reduced customer service complaint calls, less overtime, more parts produced per hour and fewer safety accidents.*

The result was a strategic effort to achieve the company's business goal of higher customer retention and increased profitability.

Measuring results

Now you know HR's job, like that of any function within an organization, is to develop strategies that impact the bottom line. But to prove that the strategies actually do impact the company's finances in a positive manner, you have to be able to show how. That means you need to speak the language of numbers.

This is why metrics—measurable, documented facts and figures—are vital in strategic HR. Measurement demonstrates HR's value to the business; to be a strategic player, HR has to keep score. And everyone can relate to numbers, regardless of personal opinions.

We'll address metrics in much more detail in Chapter 11, but it's appropriate to at least list the basic HR measures for primary areas of HR responsibility here.

Metrics for primary HR responsibilities

Organization effectiveness. Basic HR metrics can include:

Revenue factor: revenue / total employees

Expense factor: total company expense / total employees

HR expense factors: HR expense/total company expense

HR headcount ratio: total employees / HR employees

HR investment ratio: HR expense / total employees

Staffing. Basic HR metrics can include:

Cost per hire: total hiring costs / number of people hired

Time to fill: total days to fill positions / number of people hired

Time to start: total days to start / number of people hired

Offer/acceptance rate: total offers made/total acceptances

Separation. Basic HR metrics can include:

Separation rate: total separations / head count

Voluntary separation rate: total voluntary separations / head count

Voluntary separation by length of service: voluntary separations for years of service/total voluntary separations

Absence factor: [days absent/head count] / work days

Compensation and benefits. Basic HR metrics can include:

Compensation revenue factor: compensation costs / revenue

Benefit revenue factor: benefit costs / revenue

Compensation expense factor: compensation costs / expenses

Supervisory compensation percentage: supervisor compensation costs / total compensation costs

Health care factor: health program costs / total covered employees

What is HR accountable for?

Your goal is to work toward company objectives and to achieve positive business results. As a businessperson with HR as your specialty, you have distinctive talents and abilities for achieving your desired results. And that's no small task. Here is a summary of many responsibilities for which HR is accountable:

- ◆ Serving as an internal expert and advisor on both technical employment regulations and general management concepts.
- ◆ Leading the way as a change agent for organizational change and improvements.
- ◆ Asking HR's customers—top management, line managers and employees—where they're headed and how HR can help them get there.
- ◆ Developing HR strategic plans to solve business problems.
- ◆ Aligning HR resources and activities with the company's strategic objectives.
- ◆ Getting top management buy-in for HR strategic business plans.
- ◆ Communicating business objectives and strategic goals to employees whose daily efforts will ultimately lead to success.
- ◆ Implementing strategic plans and coordinating the efforts of everyone involved.
- ◆ Getting the right people with the right skills in the right place for the right price.
- ◆ Increasing employee productivity and corporate revenue.
- ◆ Providing measurable results on how HR is positively impacting the company's bottom line.
- ◆ Keeping the lid on consistently increasing HR budgets.
- ◆ Outsourcing HR functions when appropriate to budgets and strategic objectives.
- ◆ Developing your business background and skills.

Keep this list in mind so you are prepared when someone asks you, "What do you do?"

✓ Checklist

Becoming a strategic partner

☐ **Be a businessperson.** Shift the focus away from compliance in particular or HR in general and toward solving business problems. You're a businessperson whose specialty is HR.

☐ **Walk the walk.** Strategically analyze HR activities and ask your customers how you can help them. Then act on that information.

☐ **Add value.** If the HR activity doesn't add value to achieving the company's strategic objectives, don't do it.

☐ **Be proactive.** Don't wait to be proclaimed a strategic partner. Go to top management with ideas and business plans.

☐ **Share the vision.** Continually communicate business objectives and strategic goals as you work tirelessly toward the company's strategic objectives.

Unifying your HR team

Now you have to make sure everyone in HR is on the same road to executing your HR strategic plans. Less effective HR departments have some members of the HR team who understand and support the strategy, some who can recite the strategy but don't really understand it, and others who are left in the dark. This lack of mutual understanding can lead to ineffectiveness of your activities, no matter how well thought-out your strategic goals might be.

Therefore, it's important for your HR department to be unified in its goals and for everyone to understand and support your plans. You can take three steps to pull your HR people and resources together to ensure everyone is on the same road to solving business problems and helping to achieve the company's strategic objectives.

1. Put your HR strategic plan in writing

Involving your HR team members in assembling the HR strategic plan also will help them understand and take ownership of the plan. Include the following elements in your document:

- ◆ **Focus**—a summary of HR's primary business goals (such as "increase productivity by 25 percent"), core values and an explanation of how they align with the company's strategic objectives.
- ◆ **Critical measures**—balanced list of the most important performance targets that align with the company's overall performance targets and HR's primary business goals.
- ◆ **Business priorities**—agreed-upon dynamic list of the top priority projects or goals that merit immediate HR resource allocation of time, talent and money.

2. Create a connection between your HR team and the HR strategic plan

Ensuring that your HR staff is connected to your strategic plans provides a framework for efficiently managing cross-discipline teams. Put the following in writing:

- ◆ **A team contract**—clear charter of the team and focus of the team's work. This includes the evaluation criteria that will determine your expected return on HR resources allocated.
- ◆ **Deliverables**—chronological listing of specific deliverables (outcomes or goals) the HR team will produce as it reaches each milestone of the project.

3. Create an individual connection

This clarifies how much each individual contributes to the success of the HR function and what's on everyone's plate. It helps prioritize each person's activities, recognize individual performance, provide individual coaching and update individual targeted deliverables throughout the year. As a result, everyone understands how his or her role impacts strategy execution and knows how to make a difference.

For this process, it's a good idea to outline four key imperatives:

1. **Basic role.** These are critical measures developed at the HR department level to align to the individual's basic role. This clearly links individual focus with desired HR outcomes

and should contain clear, agreed-upon performance goals, competencies and measurements.

2. **Current business priorities.** This aligns your HR staff's personal goals with HR strategic business priorities and cross-discipline team accountabilities.

3. **Departments/function projects.** These are accountabilities and resources allocated to HR department activities and projects.

4. **Level and job-specific authority.** Authority is the ability to make decisions when needed. It's important to clarify and agree upon the level of authority for critical and rapid decision-making for teams and individuals.

Being a successful strategy execution leader means having meaningful discussions with top managers, top HR executives, the HR executive's peers and everyone on the HR team.

In addition, the HR manager needs to coach members of the department, while subordinates need to take responsibility for their contribution to the organization's success.

When everyone in HR understands and believes in their role in solving business problems and helping to achieve the company's strategic objectives, you'll be well on your way to being a true business partner.

DON'T miss this

❓ *The Quiz*

1. Being strategic means identifying the organization's strategic business objectives and the people capabilities needed to achieve those objectives. ❏ True ❏ False

Continued on next page

Continued from previous page

2. The key to strategic behavior is thinking first of the larger organization and its business results; you are a businessperson and HR is your specialty.   ❑ True   ❑ False

3. The difference between being tactical and being strategic is:
   a. Tactical activities affect short- to medium-term goals; strategic activities help achieve long-term objectives.
   b. Tactical approaches make incremental changes to help maintain the status quo; strategic approaches initiate changes needed for the long-term success of the company.
   c. Tactical activities generally are reactive to problems as they arise; strategic approaches are proactive in preventing problems and improving situations.
   d. All of the above

4. To make a positive bottom-line impact, the HR professional must
   a. Know and understand relevant state and federal requirements.
   b. Be knowledgeable about the company's strategic plans.
   c. Align HR strategic plans with the company's strategic objectives.
   d. Get the right people in the right place at the right time for the right price.
   e. Use metrics to measure and monitor the success of initiatives.
   f. All of the above

3. Which of the following is not a strategic responsibility for which HR is accountable?
   a. Leading the way as a change agent to solve business problems.
   b. Getting top management buy-in.
   c. Providing measurable results on how HR impacts the bottom line.
   d. Increasing the number of employees who attend training classes.
   e. Increasing employee productivity and corporate revenue.

Answer key: 1. T; 2. T; 3. d; 4. f; 5. d.

HR's dual role

As HR Director for a non-union electrical supply distributor, Michelle is responsible for more than 400 employees. She and her staff of two have some ideas for solving some of the problems they see at the company, including high turnover, low morale and low productivity in the manufacturing business unit. They also see a high absenteeism trend in the customer service department.

In addition to all that, the sales manager has approached HR and wants to clarify the definition of his exempt and non-exempt employees, which is always a challenge. And to top it all off, the CEO wants to initiate a new performance-based compensation program that likely will not please production floor workers.

Michelle keeps hearing about "getting a seat at the head table" from HR seminars, magazines, experts and peers. She'd love to be "strategic," but how does she have time for that with all the other compliance issues and problems that take up most of her time?

In recent years, the drumbeat about being strategic and "earning a seat at the table" with corporate executives has been getting louder and more urgent. For various reasons, HR professionals have hit some roadblocks along the way. This can be frustrating—after all, HR professionals know they need to think and act more strategically—but it's not surprising as the HR role continues to evolve.

WHAT you need to know

> Whether or not you have that coveted "seat at the table," in your current role as an HR professional, you know who you are and what you can do. You know you're not a police officer, lawmaker, fire fighter, accounting clerk, file clerk or scheduling assistant. But how are you perceived?
>
> These are the functions HR professionals traditionally have performed. The result is the perception that HR:
>
> ◆ Makes the rules and makes people follow them;
> ◆ Fights fires as problems arise;
> ◆ Makes sure everyone gets paid correctly;
> ◆ Keeps records on employees and helps everyone fill out forms; and
> ◆ Schedules job interviews and some company meetings.
> ◆ And don't forget the company picnic!

That's the old HR. The new HR encompasses this and a whole lot more. HR now has expanded to two roles: the traditional compliance administration activities described above, and strategic operation. Both of these functions are absolutely vital to your success as a contributing member of the strategic business team. You have to be able to perform both roles and perform them well.

First role:
Traditional compliance administration

HR's compliance administration role includes functions such as:
◆ Compensation and benefits administration;
◆ Discipline;
◆ Employee relations;
◆ Legal compliance;
◆ Payroll administration;
◆ Performance management;

- Policy development;
- Record keeping and reporting;
- Safety administration;
- Staffing; and
- Termination.

As you know, just because these functions are traditional doesn't mean they're easy. Setting up effective processes and systems for performance management, safety and human resources information systems (HRIS), for example, takes considerable planning, skill and coordination.

No matter how critical the compliance administration role is, however, you don't want to be defined by it. Instead, be defined as the individual who brings all these elements in alignment with the organization's business direction and adds to its success.

Jim Faletti, President, Strategic Insights

Every facet of compliance administration requires skilled, knowledgeable HR professionals to set up systems and processes that work well and that employees understand and trust. You and your HR team must keep up with employment laws and regulations, record keeping, staffing needs, benefits administration, technology issues and a host of other factors. The key is to perform these activities well and within the framework of the strategic operation.

Second role: Strategic operation

Despite more than a decade of talking about how HR needs to be a strategic partner, in most companies HR still is a separate island in the land of strategic involvement. To be part of the strategic operation, you need to expand your responsibilities beyond the traditional compliance administration role and participate in the highest levels of company-wide decision-making. If you're not at that level yet, it's time to start going in that direction.

> Without performing the compliance administration operations effectively, you won't be viewed as a credible strategic businessperson. After all, how can you handle "big picture" problems and initiatives if you can't handle the fundamental HR role?

Keep in mind that being part of strategic HR operations requires creative thinking. You'll use creative thinking to solve current problems, anticipate and avoid future problems, develop productivity-building initiatives, cut costs, improve morale and a host of other activities that will help the company solve its business problems.

And to solve business problems, you need to understand the business and be capable of exerting strategic influence to help achieve the company's strategic objectives.

Develop strategic influence

Think about it: In your people development function, you have the responsibility for developing workers in the same kind of dual capacity—both strategic and functional—that HR is called upon to reflect. Thinking about that functional people development responsibility of HR may help you visualize the same kind of duality to your own HR role.

DON'T miss this

Typically HR is thought of as too heavily involved in "administrative" or functional activities to be strategic. But the lack of functional expertise can be just as much of an impediment to strategic effectiveness.

In the recent past, for example, employees gained a great deal of their functional experience working in middle management and then ascended into more strategic roles. However, in the 1980s, many organizations eliminated the middle management strata and, as a result, a number of employees were catapulted into a more strategic role without having the functional experience necessary to sustain them. So don't shed your functional expertise on your way to strategic influence.

Still, influencing the organization is much more powerful than instituting policies and practices that require HR's involvement, even though those kinds of policies and practices may be necessary and appropriate. For HR to have the kind of strategic influence that truly benefits the business, it needs to be based on a belief among senior managers that better business decisions are made because of HR's input.

How do you convince senior leadership of the value of HR's input? This is accomplished by building relationships; by understanding other functional areas, their problems and needs; by knowing where the "hot spots" of problems are; and by gaining the confidence of other executives that HR's perspective will result in better business decisions.

Developing strategic influence requires you to be proactively interested in the success not only of your top executives, but also of your line managers. Line managers are a direct link to the success or failure of employees, as well as the success or failure of the company in achieving its goals. So, line managers need to see you as capable of demonstrating leadership qualities that are common to strategic leaders.

HR professionals can become strategic by helping line managers and top executives solve business problems and by helping them execute their strategies.

Most top managers want better tools and metrics to help with decision-making. They want cost reductions in HR administrative processes. They want as much efficiency as possible in compensation and benefits spending. And they want HR to perform as a strategic business partner helping to achieve the business' strategic objectives.

Much of your time will be spent addressing the functions of HR, but your perspective must never rest there. Rather, your perspective should be that of being there for all aspects of the business, focused on its success.

Understand your business

Participating in the highest levels of corporate decision-making means you have to understand the business. You should know how the company operates and what the strategic objectives are, as well as understanding basic business principles.

To operate strategically, you need a clear understanding of issues that commonly fall within the finance area. CEOs, CFOs and other top managers are recognizing the size and importance of the investment in human capital. They increasingly realize that human capital is a key factor in boosting customer satisfaction, profitability and innovation, and they want to see an analysis of the numbers and measurements that demonstrate results from their investment.

A+ *Best Practices*

Using metrics makes HR a strategic partner

Sprint uses numerous metrics that include everything from a detailed succession-planning analysis to how long it takes to fill a particular job to the dollar cost of benefits for a specific employee and his or her dependents, according to the article "The CFO Connection" by Elizabeth Smith Barnes in the July 2003 issue of *Workforce Management* magazine.

When Sprint assembles their salary budget or makes any compensation or benefits-related decision, HR knows exactly what the earnings per share impact will be. HR knows the financial implications of all HR actions and considers that knowledge part of its responsibility to the shareholders.

Setting your course directly on a business-driven approach will get you off the HR island and into the corporate mainland where you can contribute to solving business problems. To do this, you need to understand four basic principles that are true for any business:

1. **Customers should be the focus.** A business' reason for existence is to meet the current and emerging needs of its customers.

2. **Communication must be constant, honest and direct.** Management must communicate with employees, and employees must give feedback to their leaders.
3. **Leaders must plan effectively, make reasoned decisions and act.** The cost of inaction often is worse than incorrect action, so business professionals must have the confidence to take prudent risks. It's the only way to realize all of the opportunities that arise.
4. **Management and employees must operate in a culture of integrity.** Employees and managers should respect each other, as well as expect performance from each other.

Know the company's strategic objectives

A company's strategic plan should be more than a thick binder sitting on a shelf collecting dust. It must be a dynamic map to the company's future that everyone in the company uses to guide their short- and long-term activities.

Your job as a businessperson is to know and understand that strategic plan and the objectives set forth by the plan. Then communicate those objectives to your HR staff, and make sure employees and line managers understand how the programs and initiatives you lead fit into the plan.

You must always strive to solve business problems that are road-blocks to achieving the strategic objectives. Anticipating possible problems and setting forth plans to avoid them is a key function of a strategic HR partner.

DON'T miss this

Know the company's strategic positioning

Even though a company's strategic plan might be well thought-out and ingenious, the future is always uncertain. Therefore, your company can't count on a strict, specific strategic plan to enable it to achieve strategic objectives. In his Society for Human Resources Management (SHRM) white paper "Strategic HR Analysis" (© SHRM), David E. Ripley notes that instead, management must position the company with the ability to react quickly and effectively to probable and possible changes in the company's competitive environment.

Understanding the strategic plan and strategic intent. Your company's strategic plan will outline the company's intent—who you are as a company; what business you're in; where you want to be in the future; and how you want to add value in the marketplace. This plan should be the basis of all your HR planning.

Envisioning possible futures. Good strategic plans include tentative plans and preparations for unforeseen events, Ripley explains. How does your organization envision the future? Scenario planning is a good way to develop the most likely possible futures and to examine the possible business implications. It's a way to think through possible alternative futures so the company can respond more quickly and effectively to change.

Establishing strategic positions. After completing scenario planning and thinking through potential futures that they could confront, your company's strategic team can decide how to deal with those futures if they occur. Then you can determine if your company is currently positioned to take steps that might be needed. If not, you can take the actions needed to prepare the company to respond if necessary. This is called strategic positioning.

✓ Checklist

Important questions for strategic positioning

☐ What are the most likely futures developed in our scenario planning effort?

☐ How would each of these possible futures impact the way we do business in general and, specifically, in areas such as products and services, markets and resource requirements?

☐ How would each of these possible futures impact our strategic plan? Can we adapt our objectives within the framework of our current vision, mission, strategic objectives and desired culture?

☐ Are there any aspects of the operation—structure, processes, supporting systems—which need to be changed now to enable us to respond quickly to our possible futures?

David E. Ripley, "Strategic HR Analysis," SHRM White Paper, reviewed December 2002, © Society of Human Resources Management, www.shrm.org.

Once you know your company's strategic plan and key objectives, you can identify the key HR issues those plans raise. For example, does management "walk the walk" when it comes to core values? Does the organization possess the skills it needs to accomplish its strategic objectives? What is the appropriate mix of staff needed to accomplish the goals? Are the company's structure, processes and policies appropriate for where the company wants to go?

Know how your company works

No doubt you know that you must understand the business. This of course is a correct statement, as far as it goes. The problem is that it does not go far enough. Understanding the business is not a sideline to the HR role, it *is* the HR role. Understanding the business is what HR must do first, before it can do anything else.

> Knowing and understanding the business is your primary job. HR is how you deliver your strategy, the expertise that is the reason you were brought into the business.
>
> *Jim Faletti, President, Strategic Insights*

WHAT you need to know

It takes guts to take a strategic approach to HR, to focus first on knowing and understanding the business and then apply your expertise to strengthen the company's human capital. Others, particularly employees who are accustomed to a very tactical approach from their HR departments, are going to tell you—politely or not so politely—to go set up the company picnic, thank you.

Too many HR professionals want to be perceived as strategic by the other business leaders on their own terms; they want the executive group to change to accommodate them, not vice versa. This won't happen. HR needs to change its orientation to think first about the success of the business overall. This will provide the necessary framework for a strategic approach that doesn't focus on the elements of HR except as necessary to accomplish business objectives.

DON'T miss this

Knowing how your business operates doesn't mean you have to understand the intricacies of every department or business unit in your company. You simply need to understand certain core competencies and know how to focus first-line managers quickly on the issues that need to be addressed. You also can provide those managers with ideas and descriptions of your visions for where that department needs to go.

To get to know how your business works, ask managers if you can attend their staff meetings. Develop relationships with managers and exchange information and ideas about what each manager is dealing with. Find out who the informal leaders are and develop working relationships with them as well. Sometimes even going on customer calls with sales staff or technical repair staff, for example, can provide valuable insight into how HR can help a department deal with productivity, turnover and customer service.

__Example:__ In the process of trying to develop a strategic operation at the electrical supply distributor, Michelle has been asking various department managers how their departments function and what problems they face.

From several conversations with the customer service manager, who had been struggling with high absenteeism, she learned that the department's productivity had been declining for more than a year. She also learned that the employees sat in small cubicles squeezed into a dark corner of the basement.

After attending several of their department meetings, she realized that most of the employees were frustrated because their small cubicles were not set up to handle the paper flow that generated from the hundreds of phone calls and e-mails they handled each day.

Michelle then developed a business plan with the goal of reducing absenteeism by increasing morale. She proposed a plan to move the employee cubicles to a floor in the building that had windows. She outlined a workflow analysis so that their activities could be benchmarked and the offices designed to maximize their efficiency and communication with custom-

ers' sales reps. She developed metrics to show the CEO and financial officers how reducing absenteeism and increasing morale would improve productivity of the customer service employees, thus increasing customer satisfaction and helping to support sales revenue.

Comprehend basic business concepts

Because being strategic means you're a businessperson whose specialty is HR, you need to understand fundamental concepts of business and finance to help your company solve its business problems. This allows you to understand what's going on and to speak the language of business when you're interacting with executives.

This doesn't mean you have to know as much as your company's financial staff. It simply means that you need to understand the terminology and concepts so you can discuss and understand strategic plans and develop business cases for your HR initiatives. If you do happen to have an MBA or have a background working in other business units before joining HR, then you're ahead of the game.

Business laws are universal. If you understand that certain business principles are universal, then you have business acumen—the ability to focus on the basics and make money for the company.

WHAT you need to know

Every business conforms to the three basic parts of moneymaking: cash generation, return on assets and growth. You should understand these parts individually and the relationship between them. These three basic parts, plus customers, form the nucleus of any business.

1. Cash generation is the difference between all the cash that flows in the business and the cash that flows out. Cash is the lifeblood of any business.

Your CEO and financial officers are concerned with questions such as: Does the business generate enough cash? What are the sources of cash generation? How is the cash being used?

DON'T miss this

WHAT you need to know

When a business generates sufficient cash, it is in a better position to grow because the company has less dependence on borrowing money from investors.

2. Return on assets. Business leaders use either the company's money or someone else's money (for example, shareholders) to invest in the business. Whatever is invested—be it products, a "bricks and mortar" store or web site—are the business assets. In short, a businessperson always asks, "What is the return on assets?"

Earning a good return on assets has two components: profit margin and velocity. Return on assets is nothing more than profit margin multiplied by velocity. Even if profit margin is small, a business can thrive if it has a fast turnover of its inventory. A faster velocity leads to a higher return. The faster the inventory reaches the customer, the better it is for the business.

3. Growth energizes the business and creates new opportunities. However, improved margin and velocity must accompany the growth of a business, and the cash generation must be able to keep pace. Sales may be growing, but if the cash situation is getting worse, the business leaders must take a step back. Management must determine if the company is generating or consuming cash, and whether profit margin is improving or getting worse.

DON'T miss this

Business firms typically engage in five major functions:
*1. **Production of goods or services.** Usually called operations.*
*2. **Accounting and finance.** Responsible for keeping track of the money to pay suppliers, employees and stockholders.*
*3. **Marketing and sales.** Responsible for marketing and selling the product.*
*4. **Human resources.** Responsible for compliance administration and strategic operation.*
*5. **Information systems.** Usually for firms that have more than 100 employees.*

Being strategic also means taking responsibility for your own professional development. Take the opportunities whenever possible to develop your business skills, whether through conferences and seminars, college courses or degree programs, reading articles and books, or networking with peers through professional organizations.

Understand basic business terms

In addition to speaking the language of business, you actually need to understand what you and company executives are talking about or what the strategic plan really means when using the language of business. Many HR professionals hear business terms every day, but don't pay attention or assume a slight understanding from the context of how the words are used.

Take some time to familiarize yourself with basic business terms that are provided here.

Earnings	Total income minus total expenses; synonymous with profit.
Equity (also called owners' equity or shareholders' equity)	The portion of a company's assets that the shareholders own, as opposed to what they've borrowed—equal to total assets minus liabilities. Equity also is used as an adjective to describe mutual funds that invest in stocks rather than bonds.
Gross margin	Ratio of gross profit to sales revenue.
Gross profit (also called sales profit)	Sales revenue minus sales costs.
Gross revenue	The amount customers actually pay when they make their purchases, with no allowances for products expected to be returned, lost in delivery, or otherwise requiring the company to refund the customers' money.
Liability	An obligation to pay. Liabilities include accounts payable and bond and bank debt. Liability is not necessarily bad for a company—it's just an asset that they have temporary control over but don't own. If it's a useful asset and if the cost of "borrowing" it is cheap, then a liability can be a positive thing.
Operating expenses	Expenses associated with running a business but not considered directly applicable to the current line of goods and services being sold. These include sales and marketing, research and development and general administrative costs ("overhead").

Operating income	Gross profit minus operating expenses; the pre-tax, pre-interest profit from a company's operations.
Operating margin	Ratio of operating income to sales revenue.
Operations	The core activities of a business—making money by selling goods and services. Operations is considered distinct from other business activities, such as financing (raising money by issuing stocks and bonds) and investing (acquiring another company or selling off a subsidiary).
P/E ratio	The ratio of a company's share price to its per-share earnings (the current stock price divided by its earnings per share).
PEG ratio	A stock's P/E ratio divided by the annual growth rate of its company's earnings. A popular rule of thumb is that a stock is underpriced if its PEG falls much below 1, and overpriced if the PEG is much greater than 1.
Productivity (also called labor productivity or worker productivity)	Value of goods and services produced in a period of time, divided by the hours of labor used to produce them.
Profitability	The efficiency of a company or industry at generating earnings. Profitability is expressed in terms of several popular numbers that measure one of two generic types of performance: return on assets and profit margin.
Profit margin	Earnings expressed as a percentage of revenue. In other words, the percentage of sales the company has left over after paying all expenses.
P/S ratio (also called PSR)	The ratio of a stock price to its company's annual sales per share.
Quick ratio	Ratio of a company's current assets excluding inventory, to its short-term debt.
Return on assets	Earnings divided by total assets. This number expresses "what the company can do with what it's got," or how many dollars of profits they can achieve for each dollar of assets they control. It's a useful number for comparing competing companies in the same industry.
Sales costs	Expenses directly related to creating the goods or services being sold, such as the costs of raw materials or equipment depreciation. Sales costs exclude other important expenses, such as marketing and sales, research and development and interest payments on debt.

Sales revenue (also called sales, net sales, net revenue or revenue)	Income from sales of goods and services minus the cost associated with factors such as undeliverable merchandise.
Value chain	At each stage in the operation of a business, value is added by transforming some original raw input. A value chain is a set of steps in the production process that adds value to a set of inputs at each step.
Value proposition	Successful companies also need a value proposition—the organization's unique offering that sets the business apart from the competition. Among other things, it may be the process used to make products, the quality of materials, the design/look/feel factor or the customer guarantee.

Understand the corporate culture

You need a supportive corporate culture to effectively manage human capital. You need a culture in which information sharing is invited and rewarded. The answer to a key question profoundly impacts how you'll work within a culture to accomplish your strategic goals:

◆ Does management view people as an asset or a cost?

The answer to that question helps you define the scope of your approach for new initiatives. If people are viewed as an asset, your selling points for new initiatives will include the maximization of employee talents to reach company objectives.

However, if people are viewed as a cost by your top management, your persuasion techniques likely will not include the "softer" side of employee value and instead focus on how the employees' activities affect finances.

Figure out what type of culture you have

You can gauge your importance to the organization by how successfully you work within a particular corporate culture and how you help facilitate cooperation between upper-, mid- and first-line management and the work force. Corporate cultures often defy normal business strategies, so your creative and strategic thinking skills are always in demand.

WHAT you need to know

To work effectively within a culture, you need to understand the types of culture you're in. Cultures can be a combination of several influences. Some environments are derived by the ownership—family-owned, partnership, privately owned, publicly traded, etc. The number of employees also impacts the culture.

Other cultures are typical to an industry or financial setting, such as:

- ◆ Health care organizations;
- ◆ High-tech organizations;
- ◆ Manufacturing environments;
- ◆ Not-for-profit organizations;
- ◆ Professional corporations;
- ◆ Religious organizations;
- ◆ Service organizations;
- ◆ Start-ups and established companies;
- ◆ The academic sector;
- ◆ The financial sector;
- ◆ The government sector; and
- ◆ Union and non-union environments.

DON'T miss this

Corporate cultures are like fingerprints: Every company has one, and every one is different.

The corporate culture is an integral part of any business, and it can be a helpful partner to HR. However, the culture can be a source of frustration and even failure for an HR professional.

> **Example:** *Felicia is the HR Director of a small company with a casual atmosphere when a very large company purchases it. The large company has a highly professional, white-collar, suit-and-tie atmosphere and has policies to cover every minute of any operation. Felicia has no choice but to help change the culture from casual to more formal. However, she has a strong backup: the large company demands the change.*

> *Ian is in a much different situation. He has been hired with the directive to change the casual culture of a non-profit organization because the CEO thinks it's time to improve the atmosphere to professional. Ian may have an uphill battle, especially if he doesn't know how to be a change agent.*

You must decide if you want to work within the culture that exists or if you want or are hired to change the culture.

Embracing and leading change

Unless specifically given orders to the contrary by your superiors, you should get everyone involved in providing input for new ideas or processes. This usually will gain respect for HR because it shows respect for others. However, knowing who will be the likely obstacles to implementing HR changes is also a strategic necessity.

There is no substitute for getting to know the organization and how it works, just as there is no substitute for understanding its business goals and objectives. HR can't be strategic if it views itself in isolation, or if it doesn't have a true understanding for and appreciation of the individuals and departments that make up the organization. If you don't know your organization, you cannot have real strategic influence.

Meeting HR goals and evaluating their success requires a strong character, the proverbial thick skin and, most importantly, the development of alternatives to approaches that may face strong resistance.

DON'T miss this

Even with strong support from the president of a company, in-house resistance can be almost insurmountable. If resistance is strong and you haven't been assigned a specific timetable, then implementing new HR approaches can be slowed down or delayed until you gain the respect and support needed, until the "old guard" is displaced or until consensus among all employees is eventually achieved.

WHAT you need to know

Sometimes change, although unwelcome, is imperative and must be implemented immediately, without the luxury of overcoming resistance and obtaining buy-in or consensus. In times like that, you must have unity among senior leadership that change is essential to the business success; continuous communication that repeatedly illustrates how the change moves the business to where it needs to be; and brutal honesty about the impact of the changes. Don't sugarcoat the negatives (and remember, all change has some negatives).

Good communication is imperative. Communication is vital to get all employees to cooperate. Usually memos and e-mails are not the most effective way to get cooperation. If at all possible, talk to the employees before any changes are implemented and be forthright about why the changes are being made. Be sure to explain how the changes align with the company's strategic objectives. Talking, rather than using a memo, provides an opportunity for feedback and information exchange.

Be sure to communicate effectively with all members of the employee population. Make special arrangements to communicate with shift workers, part-timers and off-site employees and with employees on disability or other types of leave.

Establish credibility and dependability

It doesn't matter what kind of knowledge, talent or strategic genius you have—if you're not considered to be credible, you'll be powerless to accomplish anything and, in fact, may have a negative effect on the company's corporate culture or business programs. Your credibility and respect are characteristics that will help you persuade people, initiate programs and effectively drive change.

It's important for you to be aware of the issues that help you build trustworthiness and a reputation for dependability, as follows:

Being forthright with top management. Being credible means taking responsibility for your role as advisor to top management and being courageous enough to proceed with what you feel is right. Being a yes-man or yes-woman doesn't help you, the employees or the company.

Serving as a proactive ombudsman for employees. Most CEOs and other top managers understand the value and needs of employees. Even if some of them don't quite know how to demonstrate that "employees are our greatest asset" through their words or actions, they still believe it. They expect HR to look out for the work force—while at the same time, of course, looking out for management and the company. And that is why creative and strategic thinking is essential.

Being proactive rather than reactive. Your role is to drive change, to initiate programs and to serve as a dynamic part of the strategic planning process.

> Creative thinking is one of the best tools you have. Take the initiative to anticipate problems, anticipate opportunities and anticipate business solutions—then act on your ideas by developing business cases to show why they're necessary and follow up throughout the implementation of your plans.

WHAT you need to know

Embracing technology. For many years, HR professionals created their own roadblocks to being strategic by resisting technology. It was viewed as a threat that would eradicate their responsibilities, rather than enhance them. HR must step up and take control of knowledge management and how this technology can be used for employee self-service, efficient record keeping and training processes, and most importantly, can provide data and analysis to support the organization strategically.

Coordinating programs with other departments. You may have favorite HR-related programs and initiatives, but in other departments, such as accounting, marketing, customer service or sales, people may view those programs from a different perspective. Working with other groups in the company is vital to developing credibility and achieving your goals.

Understanding the business. If you don't understand the business, you can't work well with other groups in the company, and you can't develop strategic initiatives that are aligned with the company's strategic objectives. If you don't understand your company's operations, you'll be viewed as the stereotypical enforcer and paper-pusher—with good reason.

Being honest, open and accurate. One of the fastest and easiest ways to lose credibility—and have a difficult time regaining it—is to be perceived as dishonest, inaccurate or hiding something. In HR particularly, you have to be trusted to deliver the truth and to have your facts straight when you explain something. You must honor all commitments. You must lead by example with integrity.

Building relationships. Your success and credibility also depends on your ability to build relationships with top management, line managers, employees, vendors and industry peers. Your adeptness at forming relationships will help build trust and help people realize that you are approachable and welcome their interaction. People will see what you're made of and look to you for answers. Through your relationships, you'll also have access to opinions and information that will help you perform your job, whether getting an employee to understand the purpose of a new policy or gathering information for a business plan proposal.

Leading as a change agent. You are a primary driver of change at your company. You know what's going on with employees and with the business, and you know the company's strategic objectives. That means you know what needs to be done. And it's your responsibility to step up to the plate with a strong business case, then take a swing at hitting the "homer" your CEO needs to get the company closer to its objectives.

HR must develop and enforce workplace policies and handle all the other compliance administration functions and still take on very strategic operations.

DON'T miss this

Essentially, HR is expected to play two very different roles: to be an effective bureaucrat and a creative strategist at the same time. Your challenge is to reconcile these two converse roles within your company's particular corporate culture and stay focused on achieving the company's strategic objectives.

The Quiz

1. HR's traditional compliance administration role is still important in today's modern business. ❑ True ❑ False

2. One of HR's important roles is to help line managers and top executives solve business problems and execute their strategies. ❑ True ❑ False

3. Which of the following is not a basic component of any business?
   a. customer focus
   b. comfortable office chairs
   c. communication
   d. effective planning and reasoned decisions to act
   e. culture of integrity

4. Strategic positioning is the ability of a company to react quickly and effectively to possible changes in its competitive environment. ❑ True ❑ False

5. Knowing and understanding the business and business concepts is a key requirement to be a strategic partner. ❑ True ❑ False

Answer key: 1. T; 2. T; 3. b; 4. T; 5. T.

Building a business case

Rosa is the HR Manager for a medium-sized manufacturing firm. The CFO has asked her to review her budget and find areas to cut even more costs. In reviewing the department's operations, she decides it might be worthwhile to review their human resources information systems (HRIS). That function is currently being outsourced, but Rosa wonders if bringing those activities in-house would produce significant cost savings. How can she figure out if she could save money and if the company could handle bringing those functions inside?

You have to be a businessperson

Some people choose to be writers so they don't have to perform algebra; most construction workers prefer fresh air and sunshine to fluorescent lights and cubicles; some computer programmers avoid careers that require public speaking; and many HR professionals choose their careers to interact with people rather than for strategic planning and financial analysis.

However, it's a new world, and HR professionals today must use their knowledge and experience to help their company develop long-term strategic business plans with clear and measurable goals. Your top management won't just assume you're a strategic player who can contribute to the bottom line unless you demonstrate it by your behavior.

You have to learn your company's business. You have to be proactive and approach senior leadership with ideas and suggestions. You have to impact corporate culture, costs and revenue. HR is a key driver in the organization with the power of communicating with, motivating and developing employees.

How can you be strategic? Ask yourself, "How can I contribute to the business success of the organization?" Next, ask your internal customers how you can help them. Then be proactive with your ideas.

You and your HR staff know the most about the workforce and are already experts at adapting to rapid change. That makes your participation with company executives vital in developing a clear business approach that creates HR goals that support the company's overall strategy. This, in turn, will position you as a business partner.

Best Practices

What CEOs expect from HR

At the 2003 Society of Human Resources Management (SHRM) Annual Conference, speaker and consultant Barbara Sanfilippo of Romano & Sanfilippo listed three key characteristics CEOs say they look for from their HR leaders who want to be part of a company's strategic operations:

Act the part. Take the bull by the horns and develop a detailed HR strategic plan with a detailed budget. Ask to be included in strategic planning activities. Demonstrate how a well-coordinated strategic HR business plan can add value and income for the company.

Be proactive. Being assertive and action-oriented with your HR planning will catch the eye of the CEO and register the importance of including you in the big picture.

Be a part of the sales organization. Know the business and help foster development in the sales staff and sales function. Any company with management who knows what they're doing values the HR function. If your company doesn't see it that way, maybe it's time to find a company that will.

Speak their language

You have to be business savvy and speak the language of business. You can't work well with top management and other groups in the company if you don't have a good understanding of the business, and this understanding is vital to developing HR's credibility.

According to a 2003 study, "Human capital management: The CFO's perspective," by Mercer Human Resource Consulting, only 16 percent of the financial executives who responded said they significantly understand the return they're getting on their company's investment in human capital—compensation, benefits, training and other expenses related to the workforce. In addition, half of the financial executives reported that investors are starting to ask about human capital issues to at least a moderate extent.

This means CFOs are in a difficult situation because most see the importance of human capital to business success, but they're unable to apply ordinary financial discipline to managing what is often their company's largest investment.

That's why it's your job to translate your knowledge into action with plans that incorporate the business needs and operations of all your company's departments. HR is the most complex resource that management has to deal with. It can be difficult to quantify the softer issues such as attitude, empowerment and fairness, but you need to try to quantify them in terms of what they mean to the bottom line. And corporate leaders need language that is clear and gets to the point quickly.

WHAT you need to know

> Participating in the strategic planning process helps secure your place as an indispensable member of the business team. It's your opportunity for creative thinking and inspiration to help develop and implement useful ideas for helping employees and the company.

Researching your idea— is it a valid business case?

Take a SWOT at it!

One option for thinking through the benefits and risks of your idea is to do a SWOT analysis. SWOT stands for "Strengths, Weaknesses, Opportunities and Threats." It's a simple but useful concept. Draw four quadrants on a piece of paper or in an Excel® spreadsheet, with a vertical line and a horizontal line. Label the top left quadrant "Strengths," the top right quadrant "Weaknesses," the bottom left quadrant "Opportunities," and the bottom right area "Threats."

Strengths	Weaknesses
Opportunities	**Threats**

The top two quadrants are internal issues to the problem and the bottom quadrants are external issues. The SWOT analysis provides a quick snapshot of any situation to help develop solutions. It's important to be honest, especially with the strengths and weaknesses.

Let's look at a sample SWOT analysis for recruiting top engineers from *Fortune* 500 manufacturing firms to help with your company's product development goals. Here's what the SWOT analysis might look like:

Strengths	Weaknesses
◆ Professional; ◆ Experienced in new product development; ◆ Intelligent; ◆ Creative; and ◆ Innovative.	◆ Engineers likely arrogant, highly paid; ◆ Costs of using recruiting firm high; ◆ Relocation expenses will be incurred.
Opportunities	**Threats**
◆ ROI; ◆ Faster product-to-market; ◆ Increased customer satisfaction; ◆ Shared knowledge with current engineering staff; ◆ Increased market share; and ◆ Increased revenue.	◆ ROI; ◆ Current engineering staff could be resentful; ◆ Recruiting efforts could fail; ◆ Our company could be merged.

Doing a SWOT analysis can give you a quick view of issues you need to investigate further for your business plan.

How to determine ROI

The very first thing your CEO, CFO or other executives will look at when you present your business case likely will be the return on investment (ROI). It's one of the most important parts of your business case.

Results-based HR. This is a reflection of how HR's role has shifted from being activity-based to being results-based, according to Jack Phillips, Ph.D., of the Jack Phillips Center for Research, during his presentation at the 2003 SHRM Annual Conference.

✓ Checklist

Becoming results-based in HR

Use the following checklist to determine whether your HR department is activity-based or results-based. Moving to a results-based approach is one way HR can provide a more strategic direction to its activities.

☐ Instead of new programs being initiated whenever someone requests one, are new plans implemented only after a legitimate need is established?

☐ Instead of a multitude of programs popping up in all the departments and business units of the company, are fewer programs being implemented, but with greater opportunity to make an impact on the organization?

☐ Instead of existing programs rarely being eliminated because "they've always been here so they must be doing something right," are existing programs now regularly reviewed and eliminated when necessary?

☐ Instead of counting the number of activities, hours of involvement or number of employees involved in a program, is the program's impact on the organization now measured?

☐ Instead of limiting its involvement in the HR process, does top management get extensively involved and collaborate on many projects?

☐ Instead of HR being viewed as a cost center, is HR being viewed as an investment in a major asset—employees?

☐ Instead of HR staff operating with little or no familiarity with operations issues, must the HR staff now be very knowledgeable about operations?

☐ Instead of HR staff lacking knowledge of finance and business concepts, must HR now be versed in basic finance and business concepts?

Note the following HR applications that can be measured by ROI:
◆ Associate relations programs;
◆ Career development programs;
◆ Competency systems;
◆ Diversity programs;
◆ E-learning;
◆ Executive coaching;
◆ Executive education;
◆ Gainsharing programs;
◆ Global leadership;
◆ Organization development;
◆ Orientation systems;
◆ Recruiting strategies;
◆ Safety & health programs;
◆ Self-directed teams;
◆ Skill-based/knowledge-based compensation;
◆ Technology implementation;
◆ Total Quality Management (TQM); and
◆ Wellness/fitness initiatives.

DON'T miss this

$$Benefit/Cost\ Ratio = \frac{Program\ benefits}{Program\ costs} \qquad ROI = \frac{Net\ program\ benefits}{Program\ costs}$$

Example: *Rosa decided to submit her business plan proposing that the company bring their HRIS activities back in-house. She calculated that it would cost a total of $90,000 to transition the functions back to the company. However, she quantified the benefits of bringing it in-house to a total of $250,000.*

To figure the benefit/cost ratio, she would divide the program benefits ($250,000) by the program costs ($90,000), so $250,000 divided by $90,000 = 2.7.

Next, to figure her ROI, she needs to divide the net program benefits ($160,000, or $250,000 minus $90,000) by the program costs ($90,000). So $160,000 divided by $90,000 = 1.77; 1.77 times 100 to get a percent = 177% ROI.

How to quantify HR issues

Putting a number on topics and activities that HR deals with may seem like a daunting task, but it's simpler than you might think. You don't even have to be a financial wizard. You simply have to use some common sense and think through all the people and activities associated with an issue. Combine that with information you gather from key players in your company who can help you with your analysis.

> **Example:** *Your business plan is to eliminate or dramatically reduce sexual harassment complaints at your company. How do you quantify that for an ROI?*
>
> *Let's say that currently you get 30 complaints each year. Each complaint might incur costs for the following:*
>
> - **Productivity losses/absenteeism.** *Ask yourself, how much time did the complainant spend away from productive work? Was there any sick time involved? Also, how many employees were interviewed in the investigation of the complaint? Using those employees' hourly pay rates, you can establish the cost of productive time lost.*
> - **HR/EEO staff time.** *Similarly, how much of your HR or EEO staff's time was taken in the investigation and complaint resolution procedure?*
> - **Management time.** *Don't forget to include the costs of management time, both in the investigation and resolution but also time spent briefing upper management on the complaint's progress.*
> - **Legal fees.**
> - **Settlements/losses.**
> - **Direct expenses associated with the legal process.**

So you add up all the costs associated with these elements to get a total of, say, $725,000 annually. That's how much you could save the company each year by eliminating sexual harassment complaints. In addition, you now know that each complaint costs your company $21,750 ($725,000 annual total cost divided by 30 complaints per year).

Another common HR issue that many professionals view as difficult to quantify is the cost of turnover. Sure, you can easily cite your turnover percentage. But do you know how much it costs your company? Knowing that can underscore the importance of a business plan you want to propose.

> **Example:** *You're having a problem retaining middle managers in the manufacturing operations—they seem to be leaving at an increased rate over the past year. You want to propose a plan to increase middle management retention and to develop their skills and leadership potential. That means you need to know how much it costs the company when a middle manager leaves. How do you quantify that?*
>
> *First, look at an average middle manager's annual salary in the manufacturing and production business unit—$80,000. Now take into consideration staff time and direct costs associated with recruiting, hiring, orientation and training to get that replacement person up to speed—$35,000. That means the total cost of turnover per employee is $115,000, or 144 percent.*

Every company will have some non-quantifiable, intangible benefits to include in their explanation of ROI and benefits of their business plan. Some of them can include:

- ◆ Increased job satisfaction;
- ◆ Increased organizational commitment;
- ◆ Improved teamwork;
- ◆ Improved customer service;
- ◆ Reduced complaints;
- ◆ Reduced conflicts and hostility; and
- ◆ Reduced stress.

What the ROI process can do besides give you numbers

Successfully using the ROI process as an integral part of your business plans will show your company leaders that you understand the importance of all parts of the business to its financial success. You can use the ROI to:

- ◆ Show contributions of selected HR programs.
- ◆ Identify inefficient programs that need to be redesigned.
- ◆ Identify successful HR programs.

Having a business focus to your HR objectives, demonstrated by understanding and effectively tracking ROI, will, in addition, likely gain confidence of other functional areas and improve support for HR overall.

Keep in mind, however, that merely calculating an ROI does not guarantee that your business plan will be approved. In addition, some possible dilemmas can arise regarding the ROI process:

- The time to pursue the ROI is when you don't have time to pursue it.
- The ROI process is not a quick fix.
- If the HR staff does not see the need for ROI, it usually will fail.
- Without cooperation of participants contributing information during the ROI process, it usually will fail.
- Without the support of management and their sincere belief in the credibility of your ROI calculations, the process usually will fail.
- A variety of groups, such as line managers, individual departments or your own HR staff, must learn about the ROI process.

What are the elements of a business plan?

Now it's time to prepare your report for top management and other key players. The process of developing a business plan is true strategic planning—you develop an hypothesis for short- and long-term objectives, define your perspective on the problem or situation, develop a theory for the solution, then develop empirical evidence to see if it supports your theory.

Armed with that information, you develop a business plan. This is an integral tool for today's HR professional—it outlines the direction your department will take to operate. This should be a practical outline of what you need to have, not a wish list. A typical business plan will include the following:

- Executive summary;
- Subject and scope;
- Long- and short-term objectives;
- List of benefits;

◆ Criteria and constraints;
◆ Alternatives;
◆ Risks and contingencies;
◆ Competitors, if applicable;
◆ Long- and short-term financial forecasts; and
◆ Recommendations and conclusions.

Let's examine these elements in more detail.

Executive summary

We all know at least one busy company executive who doesn't have either the time or the desire to read an entire report, no matter how brilliant that report may be. The executive summary recaps your plan so your corporate leaders can quickly learn about what you want, what the budget is, who will be involved and what the benefits will be to the company.

Your executive summary should include:

◆ **Brief description of the subject and scope.** Summarize the project in one to two sentences.
◆ **List of objectives.** Make the list brief and don't include explanations of each objective.
◆ **List of benefits.** Again, make the list brief and don't include explanations. Include the ROI.
◆ **Summary of costs.** Don't explain how the costs were calculated—simply provide the totals.
◆ **Summary of resources needed.** Briefly list the people, time and other resources required for the plan.
◆ **Summary of risks.** Provide a succinct, straightforward list.
◆ **Bottom-line financial forecasts.** Again, simply provide the totals, not the calculations involved.
◆ **Recommendations.** State clearly and directly in one to two sentences what action you recommend the HR department and company take.

Following the executive summary, the full text of your report begins. Although you still need to write concisely, this is where you can explain important details of your plan.

Subject and scope

When defining your business plan and the breadth of activities, remember to use the language of business that financial officers and CEOs prefer and understand. Don't use flowery adjectives or describe pie-in-the-sky ideas. Refer to specific situations and facts, not ideas.

Anticipate the questions your company leader will have, such as:

◆ What is the concept?
◆ Why is it needed?
◆ How will it fit into the company's overall business strategies?
◆ How will the plan work?
◆ Who will benefit?
◆ What are advantages of the plan?
◆ What are limitations of the plan?
◆ How will success be measured?

Long- and short-term objectives

Any plan, large or small, has to have a purpose. Clearly define the goals and anticipated outcomes of your plan. Answer questions such as:

◆ Why is this plan needed?
◆ What are the issues you're facing in the organization that prompted HR to develop this plan?
◆ How do those issues affect the company's strategic plans?
◆ What are the opportunities created by the plan?
◆ What specifically do you hope to accomplish?

Your executives will appreciate your focus on business success, which is what a strategic partner does, when you show them you think in both the short term and the long term. Make sure you outline immediate goals (first two to three years) as well as strategic future goals (three to five years).

Remember to define objectives based on facts, not ideas.

Benefits

Describing benefits of the business plan is different than listing the objectives. A benefit is a result of achieving an objective. For example, an objective can be to reduce turnover by 20 percent; an anticipated benefit of that objective would be reducing current costs for recruitment, hiring and training by 15 percent.

DON'T miss this

Describing benefits of the business plan is different than listing the objectives of the plan. A benefit is a result of achieving an objective.

In this section of your business plan, answer questions such as:

◆ **What will the benefits be?** What issues will the plan resolve? What will be the ROI? Remember to use the language of business—quantify the benefits.

> **Example:**
> **Bad:** *Save money on computer software.*
> **Good:** *Reduce costs of upgrading computers by $100,000.*

Determining the ROI is a key element to the success or failure of your business case. It is an important HR evaluation tool, and your corporate executives will want to see it.

◆ **Costs.** Itemize all costs, both indirect and direct. Include factors such as database downtime, productivity stoppages or other situations that will reduce resources during the plan's implementation.

Different types of costs exist for different activities, so be sure to include all applicable costs in your analysis. Categories for costs include:

◆ Analysis costs.
◆ Development/acquisition costs.
◆ Implementation costs.
◆ Operating costs.
◆ Evaluation costs.

Remember that costs and resource allocations must be less than the benefits of your plan. CEOs are cautious about making mistakes, and financial officers are diligent in examining all angles of a project's financial scope.

◆ **What are opportunities?** Address potential for cost savings, productivity increases, revenue growth, customer satisfaction, employee satisfaction, enhanced employee skill sets to meet company goals, etc.

Remember to use the language of business—facts, numbers and specifics.

Criteria and constraints

This is the section of the report for describing what it will take to get your plan done and outlining the schedule for all project elements. This section will be of special interest to your company's financial officers.

The elements to include are:

Implementation schedule. When setting up the schedule, be sure to consider factors such as:

◆ **Holidays, vacations, work travel and other schedule considerations** of key personnel involved.

◆ **Corporate and legal review and approval processes** needed for any part of the project. Such reviews, whether performed by your own company or outside organizations involved in the plan, can take considerable time.

◆ **Your company's fiscal year and budgeting process.** It would not be wise to present a business case in July for implementing your plan next year when, for example, your company just finalized next year's budget in June and it's too late to add your plan to it.

Also make sure that you schedule expenses, resource purchases (such as new equipment), software installation and upgrades, recruiting activities or other actions at appropriate times of the year for your company's and your industry's business cycles.

- ◆ **Busy and slower times in your company's business cycle.** Knowing when resources will be at full capacity can help you develop a realistic timetable.
- ◆ **Major tradeshows or other industry events for your company.** You don't want to plan key initiatives if you need employees easily accessible for communications or other activities of the project.

Major milestones. Each of your objectives should have a series of goals to achieve in reaching the main objective. Identify key goals as major milestones and highlight those. This will help everyone involved, especially top management, see the progress as your plan moves along.

Major dependencies. What people, events and other factors are essential to the successful completion of your business plan? Are there any factors that could stop the plan if they change?

Resources. This is the area to describe the money, people and time needed for your plan. Which departments within the company will incur costs? What personnel will be involved, and how much time will they devote to this project? Include information about who, both company employees and outside persons, will be involved in carrying out your program. How many hours, weeks, months or years will be devoted to completing the plan?

Budget. Develop a realistic budget based on facts, not ideas. Include both direct and indirect costs, as well as any source of revenue. Talk with your financial department staff to ask how to present the budget and what factors to include.

This also is an excellent opportunity to partner with your key financial staff. In the process of obtaining their advice on how to best approach the budgeting process, you'll form alliances with your business partners and increase your perceived value as an essential business partner for your company.

Quality issues. Explain the factors and actions that are necessary to maintain the desired quality level for your business plan.

For example, if one of your action items is to recruit top engineers from *Fortune* 500 manufacturing firms to help your company meet its product development strategic goals, explain how those top level employees are essential to achieving your objectives and why lesser experienced engineers would not be suitable.

Technology. Describe the technology needed to implement the plan. Talk with your IT staff for insights into technical requirements and limitations in achieving your objectives. The best business plan in the world can shatter in seconds if appropriate technology considerations are not examined thoroughly.

Working with your technical staff is another chance to form alliances with your business partners and enhance your value as a strategic partner.

Alternatives

A good business case is not complete without an analysis of alternatives. In thinking through your project, consider different ways to achieve your objectives if your plan doesn't work as anticipated.

Your plan will, of course, contain what you believe to be the best options for achieving your goals. When allowing for alternatives, you can consider the less-than-perfect but workable options that might not be your preference, but which would likely still help you successfully complete the project.

In addition to choices for completing the plan, include the obvious alternative of doing nothing. It may sound odd, but doing nothing is always an alternative. What happens if you do not implement your business plan? Will costs continue to rise in certain areas? Will key personnel likely leave the company? Will the company be at risk of losing confidential information to competitors? Will the organization be at risk of violating employment laws? Or, will nothing bad happen? Whatever the situation will be if nothing is done, outline those circumstances.

Risks and contingencies

Be candid in listing the risks associated with completing your plan. CEOs and other top executives know that risk-taking is essential to entrepreneurial growth and leadership, and risks are expected. Your credibility won't be at stake for stating possible problems; however, your credibility may be at stake if you don't plan for and communicate the possible dangers.

You also need to plan for factors outside your control that could affect your project. What if the economy bottoms out and your company's revenue follows suit? What if your company is sued for an employment-related issue and requires a significant portion of time from key players, including you? What if the union goes on strike? What if your company is purchased and the organization's client base suddenly changes so that you no longer need those high-level engineers? Try to think of all possible, realistic roadblocks and changes, and then develop alternatives to address those contingencies.

Financial forecasts

Present your business case's financial forecasts in a P&L (profit and loss) format and other ways that your top management prefers to see the numbers. You'll need to coordinate with your company's financial staff to ask for suggestions on how to prepare the information appropriately.

Recommendations and conclusions

This section should clearly state the conclusions you draw from all the previous information, and your realistic recommendations based on those conclusions. For example, perhaps you determined that spending $75,000 annually to outsource your payroll function would save $110,000 annually in direct costs and 400 hours of staff time at an average of $21 per hour ($8,400). So, recommend that your company outsource the payroll function.

Did you conclude that spending a one-time fee of $100,000 for a recruiter to find three top *Fortune* 500 engineers with $125,000 salaries would bring in $3,500,000 in new revenue over the next four years? Then consider recommending that your company recruit those engineers.

Creating an HR scorecard

To evaluate your business case, you can create a "human resources scorecard" that generates six types of information to help you evaluate the business plan:

♦ **Reaction to the HR program.** Will there be any productivity slowdowns? Will employee communication pieces or meetings be needed? Anticipate and measure participant satisfaction. Examine any resources that should be devoted to employee and management reaction to your business plan's implementation.

♦ **Learning skills/knowledge.** Anticipate and measure changes in knowledge, skills and attitudes.

♦ **Implementation progress.** What did and didn't work? Measure changes in on-the-job behavior or actions as the program is applied.

♦ **Business impact related to HR program.** How has your plan influenced the corporate culture, costs and revenue? Anticipate and measure changes in business impact variables.

♦ **ROI.** Your proposal contained your anticipated ROI. Now, what is the actual ROI?

♦ **Intangible benefits.** You'll almost always find benefits that cannot be quantified, such as increased job satisfaction, improved teamwork or reduced conflicts. However, these are important to the company's success and should be included in your evaluation.

You can use this human resources scorecard to determine the ROI after the business plan has been implemented as well. It's imperative to do a post-implementation evaluation, both to sharpen your personal strategic analytical skills and to evaluate the success of your projects.

?²The Quiz

1. HR professionals can be strategic by thinking about how they can impact their organization, asking their customers for input and being proactive.
   ❏ True   ❏ False

2. Participating in the strategic planning process:
   a. Helps secure your place as an indispensable business partner.
   b. Provides the opportunity for creative thinking.
   c. Helps develop employees.
   d. Helps achieve strategic company objectives.
   e. All of the above.

3. HR professionals have to be financial wizards to be capable of quantifying HR issues and determining ROIs when preparing a business case.
   ❏ True   ❏ False

4. An executive summary of a report should include concise information on the business plan's subject and scope, objectives, benefits, criteria and constraints, alternatives, risks, financial forecasts and recommendations and conclusions.
   ❏ True   ❏ False

5. CEOs and other top managers know that risk-taking is essential to entrepreneurial growth and leadership, and it helps establish the HR professional's credibility to point out risks to any business plan.
   ❏ True   ❏ False

Answer key: 1. T; 2. e; 3. F; 4. T; 5. T

Getting top
management buy-in

Melissa has just been hired to be the HR Director for an international chemical manufacturer. One of her first goals is to change the current HR department from a paper-pushing, activity-based operation to a creative thinking, results-oriented department. However, she doesn't know anything about chemical manufacturing, since her work experience is in the retail industry. And she certainly doesn't have any experience in sales. How can the HR department impact the sales and cost savings for a complex operation such as chemical manufacturing? If HR has some ideas, who at the company can help them figure out if the ideas will work? Then, how do they convince top management these ideas will work or at least get a fair hearing for them?

How to get approval

You can have fantastic ideas for strategic HR programs that are aligned with the company's strategic initiatives, but if you can't convince the CEO and other top executives to proceed, your ideas won't mean anything. Learning to develop and present programs for approval is one of the most important goals for HR professionals.

HR efforts can't be implemented effectively unless top management values and supports the HR activities at your company. This requires a management philosophy that values employees, invests in HR, has a commitment to careful development and evaluation of HR practices, and involves HR in strategic planning activities.

Factors in obtaining approval

Factors that determine HR's ability to be proactive in getting approval for strategic business plans include:

◆ Your relationship with the CEO.
◆ Your relationship with key (official and unofficial) leaders and corporate executives.
◆ The corporate culture.
◆ The amount of change your business plan will create.
◆ The costs of your plan.
◆ Your credibility as a business leader.
◆ Timing.
◆ The effectiveness of presenting your business plan.

DON'T miss this

The key to achieving a successful HR strategic business case is to make sure your plan solves a business problem.

If your business case solves a problem without incurring unrecoverable costs, it usually will sell itself. Every executive wants to succeed and wants help doing it. You'll have a distinct advantage if you find out what kinds of issues keep your executives up at night, and then address those issues in your business case. You'll get more approvals than rejections and earn your place as one of your organization's strategic business partners.

Develop a relationship with the CEO

Before you can build a relationship with your president or CEO, you have to know who he or she is. Where did your CEO work before joining your company? What is her background? What is he enthusiastic about? What are the CEO's likes and dislikes? What's his or her hidden agenda? What is his or her work style? What kind of people is the CEO close to?

In the July 1993 *Workforce Management* magazine article, "Selling HR: How to Get CEO Support," Peggy Stuart noted that high-level leaders tend to have three common characteristics:

- ◆ **They are strategists and visionaries.** They may view the world from different perspectives, and they'll view your business plan through the glasses of that vision.
- ◆ **Their job is constantly on the line.** Every decision he or she makes affects job security; this has an incredible impact on motivation. Keep that in mind when you develop and present a business case.

- ◆ **They are "big picture" people.** Living with risk means the CEO is more likely to prefer long-term conclusions to the details of how those conclusions were reached. This means that your presentation must separate issues and put them into the big picture perspective for management.

Know the CEO's background. Knowing your CEO's work experience is important in helping you figure out how to present your business plan. For example, if the CEO has an engineering background, you'll want to include a flow chart, Gantt chart, cost summary or other tools he or she is accustomed to working with. A background in finance may require a generous use of numbers. If he or she has a background in sales, he'll recognize any tricks you try to use to be too smooth and convincing.

> **Example:** Melissa is working on her business plan for the chemical manufacturing company, and she has learned that the CEO, Phil Wickert, has a reputation for resisting new ideas until they can be proven to have a high likelihood of being successful. So Melissa wants to learn what concepts and tools Mr. Wickert tends to favor when making decisions.
>
> A couple weeks after starting her job, she invited Mr. Wickert to a "get acquainted" lunch. She found him cordial and learned that he was involved in a range of activities outside the office, including golf, boating and collecting World War II guns and ammunition. She learned that he got into collecting war memorabilia when he was the VP of Finance at a metal manufacturing company that supplied gun parts and components to gun manufacturers. It was at that time that he combined his interest in WWII (because of his father's service) with his interest in the arms industry in which he worked.
>
> Knowing about his background in finance at a metals company, Melissa designed her business plan to include common financial analyst tools—a workflow chart, a cost summary, bar charts and an ROI summary—as well as several metaphors involving guns or metal to illustrate her points about her plan.

Know how the CEO thinks. Be a good listener and find out which key topics this CEO will listen to when anyone wants his attention. Every leader has certain issues that are key, "hot-button" goals. Recognizing what these key issues are for your CEO is helpful to getting your business cases approved.

WHAT
you need
to know

> You can discern a lot by being a keen observer. Notice if he or she interrupts conversations or moves someone along in a conversation. At what points or topics does the CEO listen politely as opposed to being engaged? When does she change the subject? Listen to which issues get his full attention—profits? Cost cutting? Stock prices? A certain department in your company? Humor? Find out, and then build your presentation around those topics and situations.

Example: *A CEO is known for his keen business sense, but he's not exactly known as a "people person." He can analyze a new work/life benefit program, but he has no interest in the "touchy feely" part of communicating and implementing such programs. Knowing this, the HR Director's proposal for a new wellness program emphasizes the HR department's role in setting up an employee communication plan for the project and for providing counseling service referrals for employees. The CEO is more than happy to let HR handle those activities that he doesn't prefer, while he and the CFO monitor the program's positive impact on the company's bottom line.*

Know the CEO's communication style. Observe how long he'll listen to someone talk before he feels the need to speak. See if she has sidebar conversations during meetings while someone else is talking. Does he or she tend to be quiet or gregarious during meetings? Getting a feel for the boss' communication style allows you to blend with that style and communicate effectively. For example, your communication style may be direct, and you may prefer to get an answer as soon as you present your plan. However, if your executive doesn't make quick decisions, he may put your issue lower on the priority list if you try to rush him.

Know the CEO's work style. Is the CEO an action person or a bottom-line person? Is he or she excited about the long-term effects of a plan and not just the highlights? Does he or she want a one-page memo or a comprehensive report? Is the CEO a better listener in the office or at a restaurant? Is he a morning person? HR professionals should modify their work style to blend with the work style of the president or CEO in order to communicate most effectively.

DON'T miss this

This doesn't mean you should become a yes-man or yes-woman. Credibility is vital to the acceptance of your business plan. For HR to be credible, you have to take responsibility for your actions and your proposals, and that can mean taking bad news to top management. HR's role is to advise, but be prepared to move on if your proposal is rejected and implement whatever decision is made.

Foster relationships with other key players

Although your relationship with the CEO is critical, it's not the only game in town. In fact, if your HR department doesn't have much credibility as a strategic advisor to the business, it might make more sense to start building influence with other key leaders first.

Get key people on board. Spend time building agreement and support with people below the CEO, including people in the CEO's inner circle. It also helps to have good relationships with unofficial leaders and key players at the company—people who might not have an executive title but who know what's going on, who have management's ear, or who have ideas that can help you.

WHAT you need to know

Researching and preparing information for your business plan is the perfect opportunity to foster those relationships while building understanding and support for your plan.

If you don't already have good working relationships with key managers in the financial, operations, manufacturing and other business units of your company, it's time to start developing them. Be sincere, and be proactive. Ask about how things are going in their functional units. Learn about their functional responsibilities and their most pressing needs; ask how HR might be able to help. Attend staff meetings to get to know their people, how they operate and what their goals are.

Develop these relationships over time. Then when you're preparing a business plan, discuss ideas and get feedback about your business case. This allows you to get a feel for the potential success of your business plan without anyone committing to the plan.

Get to know each person over breakfast, lunch, dinner or some other informal atmosphere. Psychologically, people feel more comfortable in a casual atmosphere instead of in front of a big desk.

DON'T miss this

Example: *In the process of developing her business case, Melissa realized that she was so new to the company she didn't know what kind of information the CFO liked to have for projects. She contacted the finance department to find out what kind of information to include in her analysis and how to format the information. She ended up meeting with Earl Lexington, who reports to the CFO. Although Earl's boss, and not Earl himself, would be the one in the meeting when Melissa made her presentation, Earl was extremely knowledgeable about what kind of information the CFO looks for and how she should format her financial statements—after all, he had worked at the company for more than 16 years. In the course of the meeting, they drifted into casual conversation about family, friends, hobbies and what it was like to work at the company.*

After the meeting, Melissa knew she'd made an important contact, and a week later invited Earl to lunch. Two weeks after that, at the company picnic, she chatted with Earl's wife and played ring-toss with his daughter. When they were packing up to leave for the day, Earl mentioned that he'd been thinking and thought it would be a good idea for Melissa to include the cost of employee turnover in the customer service department in her business plan. This advice helped her prepare a more thorough analysis.

One helpful strategy is to get a respected member of top management to sponsor your business plan. This person can help you develop your case, then help you during the presentation. Make this advocate part of the process of preparing the plan and presentation. Also, that sponsor can let you know if you're off base with any part of your plan before you present it formally to the CEO.

Be politically savvy

Keep in mind that politics is a dangerous game in any work environment. It's important to take an intuitive approach. One effective approach is to sit back and listen. You'll want to know who the power brokers are. Once you know that, you can move forward in a certain direction, especially if you're competing for time and attention with other HR directors, as can be the case in larger corporations.

Understand the corporate culture

Your company's corporate culture will influence how the organization handles your business plan's implementation. It's vital to understand and account for your culture and make sure your plan will fit within it, rather than fight against it.

For example, if you have an open culture in which employees are used to open discussions and consensus building, your approach will be different than the approach needed for a closed, autocratic corporate culture in which decisions are made from the top down.

Stuart's *Workforce Management* article, "Selling HR: How to Get CEO Support," suggests that you ask yourself these questions:

◆ **Where is the power in the organization?** Analyze any underlying problems or folklore that exist and need to be overcome. Also consider any employees who are power brokers and influential with groups of other employees. Include these factors in your plan and involve people in communicating about the project.

◆ **How does management function?** Know whether managers rely on committees for decisions, if specific individuals make decisions, or if decisions are delegated to a lower level. If your company has a board of directors, understand its role in decision-making as well.

If the real decision-maker isn't the CEO, focus on the person who does make decisions. Maybe it's the vice president, the CFO, the chairman of the board or someone else. The best strategy may be to work through that person.

Stuart points out that corporate culture is also reflected in the role of HR within the company. Paper-pushers and number-crunchers who sit and wait for problems to land on their desk inhabit some HR departments. When problems arise, they react, then return to waiting for the next problem.

Other HR professionals participate in strategic planning with the CEO and other members of top management. Their HR functions are always at least one step ahead of the rest of the organization—analyzing, predicting and designing programs for problems that haven't come up yet. Problems are stopped or slowed before they have a chance to get too big. Where the company culture allows it, this approach is infinitely preferable.

Be a change agent

Trying to implement new HR programs in support of a business strategy sometimes can be like trying to parallel park a cruise ship. Change means that people have to leave their comfort zone or lose control. Resistance to change is a difficult roadblock that many new HR programs face—from top management's reluctance to employees' resistance during implementation.

Nevertheless, change is inevitable. It's often HR's role to determine what the change should be, communicate it to top management and gain approval, then communicate it effectively to employees and implement that plan while ensuring that the change will have a positive effect on the company's business success.

WHAT you need to know

Projects that have a wide impact across the entire organization can be especially difficult to sell. In today's business environment, however, many programs aren't appropriate for the whole company. Individual departments or business units typically need their own structure, so you probably won't have as many across-the-board programs as you might have had 10 or 15 years ago.

Justify the costs of your plan

No business case will be approved if the benefits don't outweigh the costs. Everyone is cost-sensitive, and companies go out of business all the time. Mergers and acquisitions, bankruptcies, increased competition domestically and overseas and tough economic times add extra pressure to the CEO and top management.

If you're proposing a program with a high price tag, make sure you've thoroughly researched the expenses and can justify spending the money for the outcome anticipated.

DON'T miss this

Most worthwhile programs will cost money and/or take up the time of employees, so it's best to assume that it will be hard to get approval. But don't give up—do your homework and be prepared.

Establish credibility as a business leader

As discussed in Chapter 3, HR professionals must use their knowledge to help develop long-term strategic business plans with clear and measurable goals. You'll establish credibility as a business leader when you not only effectively take care of the critical administrative and compliance issues, but also when you contribute to the company's bottom line.

You have to know your company's business first in order to impact corporate culture, costs and revenue. That means you will not propose plans without cost analysis and benefit evaluations. It means you will budget based on facts, not ideas. It means you do not want to be just a paper-pusher. It means you want to be proactive in searching for opportunities to solve the company's problems.

You also gain credibility by being proactive rather than reactive. This requires creative thinking—one of the most important skills of a successful strategic HR professional. Avoid thinking about HR simply as a rule-making and enforcing function. Top managers are looking for creative problem solving, creative problem avoidance and creative strategic initiatives.

> **Example:** *Employer A set up an equal employment opportunity (EEO) program as a way to avoid legal liability. Employer A's focus was pure compliance with government regulations.*
>
> *Employer B established a program to attract a diverse work-force and create a bridge to minority communities that will make up an increasing population of the work force. Compliance with government regulations was a result of Employer B's actions, but not its focus.*
>
> *Employer A was being reactive to a present need—a tactical approach. Employer B was being proactive in anticipating future needs—a strategic approach.*

Get the timing right

When you present your proposal can be just as important as the *content* of your presentation. If you don't have top management's full attention, you're wasting your time. If you request a budget, but your company just closed its budget cycle, you're wasting your time and hurting your credibility by not knowing the budget timetable. Time your presentation so that it gets attention and so that its costs and effects fit into the bigger picture of other major events.

Example: *In 1992, the HR team at a plastics factory proposed that the company establish a smoke-free environment. The first time they made the presentation, the idea was rejected. The CEO said the company would be infringing on the rights of workers by telling them they couldn't smoke in the workplace. The HR team accepted the decision but still believed in the concept, so they researched the effects of second-hand smoke. They also researched the smoking policies of employers in their area.*

In 1993, the U.S. government, as well as independent researchers, released the results of studies on the effects of second-hand smoke. The plastics factory's HR department already had the documentation and presented the new policy proposal again. This time, it was approved.

✓ Checklist

Timing considerations for scheduling the proposal meeting

- ☐ Annual meetings
- ☐ Board of Directors meetings
- ☐ Other key company meetings
- ☐ Upcoming mergers & acquisitions
- ☐ Key industry tradeshows & conferences
- ☐ Company's budget cycle
- ☐ Planned reductions in force
- ☐ Pending law or regulation changes
- ☐ Holidays
- ☐ Vacation time of key participants
- ☐ Travel schedules of key participants

Make an effective presentation

You should lay the foundation for proposing any business case before you're ready to make your presentation, so that it's no surprise to anyone. At this point you've been developing working relationships with the CEO and other key players, so make sure they are aware of the concept before the official presentation occurs.

> The content of your presentation should not be a surprise; it should be your opportunity to inform and persuade the key players to accept your business case.

WHAT you need to know

The presentation also is your opportunity to get the CEO to own the idea. This will help ensure his or her support and the support of the employees and board of directors.

Request the proposal meeting. The first step is to request a meeting to make the presentation. Only you know how you best communicate with your CEO and other members of top management. You may want to request the meeting through a verbal request; you may want to prepare a memo to request the meeting; you may want to do a combination of both. How you request the meeting is up to you. Emphasize that the meeting is for discussion purposes and that you are not expecting an immediate decision at that meeting.

Remember that in getting to know your CEO, you should have learned in what environment he or she best listens, such as office meetings, informal lunches or formal dinners. Try to arrange your meeting in the best place for getting the boss' attention.

Meld your communication style. Remember to use what you know about the CEO and other key players and how they think to choose your communication style prior to the presentation. That doesn't mean you have to be an imposter and not be yourself; it simply means that you need to know how best to communicate with these key players so that your message will be heard and understood.

Keep the presentation as short as possible. Remember that the CEO's time is a precious commodity. Don't worry about being entertaining; concentrate on being quantitative and persuasive.

Review the main points. During your briefing, summarize the key facts, objectives and recommendations. Leave the details for the executives to read in your report or ask about after you finish your presentation. You don't want the CEO cutting you off while you're making your presentation—that means it's taking too much time, and he or she likely has stopped listening.

While presenting your summary, however, it's important to be thorough. Stress the program's benefits and well thought-out recommendations. Explain how the plan will benefit both the company and employees.

Use the language of business. As discussed in Chapter 3, it's important for you to use the language of business—business terms related to financial statements, workflow analyses and other quantitative impacts of softer HR issues. Financial officers, for example, will want numbers and will let you do the worrying about how people will respond emotionally.

Prepare the room ahead of time. Go to your meeting room several hours or more before your meeting to make sure everything is set up the way you want it—chairs, lights, refreshments, handouts and anything else you feel is important for the meeting.

Also make sure the audio-visual equipment is working and that you know how to operate it. Your brilliant idea will be lost and your credibility will be negatively affected as executives sit and watch you try to figure out how to get your computer to boot up or your overhead projector to turn on.

Use visuals that are appropriate. Whether you use a single overhead slide or a sophisticated PowerPoint® presentation, use presentation visuals that are appropriate both for your audience and for the information you're trying to convey. Don't over-complicate simple information by trying to include fancy animated graphics in your computer slide show, but also don't over-simplify complex information by putting multiple concepts on one slide.

If possible, ask your marketing staff for tips on how to prepare the visuals. If you don't have access to employees who know how to prepare presentations, talk to your peers through associations or societies to which you belong. You can also find a myriad of sources on the Internet.

Allow two-way communication. Part of communication is listening, so pay attention to everything said by the CEO and other key players in the meeting. You may be able to get a clearer picture of what they feel is important or have concerns about, so bring a lot of backup material. Depending on your plan's potential impact, you may need to have many reports available at the meeting to support your case.

Be prepared for questions. Put yourself in the CEO and CFO's shoes and anticipate questions based on *their* perspectives. Then have your answers ready. Preparing answers for all possible questions ahead of time will help ensure you've thought through the business plan.

Remember that questions are not an attack. The executives simply need to improve their understanding so they can make informed decisions.

Sometimes, even the best presentations and greatest ideas will be rejected. That's a normal part of doing business. Presenting a new idea always involves some level of risk. Take rejections in stride and move forward to your next idea.

Effective change requires trust

For any changes, big or small, HR's role is to first establish a relationship of trust—especially with your CEO. Without trust, employees will think you're trying to take advantage of them every time you try to make a change. This is when the credibility discussed in Chapter 2 comes into play.

When your plans are approved and it's time to implement, your role as a change agent is essential. All eyes will be on you—how you lead, how you work with teams, how you interact with individuals, how you handle problems that come up along the way, and how you communicate.

DON'T miss this

How you make people feel and how organized and logical your implementation plans are will affect your personal and professional credibility. It also will affect how management and employees perceive your future plans.

Get employee buy-in after the plan is approved

When an HR department introduces a new program, company buy-in is imperative for the program to be successful. If the entire organization is prepared for change and is informed of progress along the way, the company will continue to perform productively during and after the program's implementation. Everyone involved needs to believe in the program.

✓ Checklist

Rules for attaining employee buy-in

- ☐ Ensure that everyone involved in the effort is committed to the program's purpose and is working toward a common goal.
- ☐ Develop a sense of team spirit among those involved, and see that it prevails throughout the program's development and implementation.
- ☐ Provide constant, regular communication for everyone involved.
- ☐ Reinforce the idea that nothing really is a mistake, but instead is a learning experience.
- ☐ Ensure that no one places blame on others for problems. Instead, emphasize solving problems.
- ☐ Watch for stress symptoms and talk openly about feelings and concerns.

Source: "How HR Attained Company Buy-In for Its Internship Program," Shannon Peters, Workforce Management, September 1993.

The Quiz

1. Which of the following factors does not affect your ability to get approval for your business plans?
   a. Your relationship with the CEO.
   b. Your relationship with key leaders and corporate executives.
   c. Your credibility as a business leader.
   d. The effectiveness of presenting your business plan.
   e. The corporate culture.
   f. Your ability to bake good brownies for the company food day.
   g. The amount of change your business plan will create.
   h. Timing.

2. Which of the following is not a common characteristic of CEOs?
   a. They're strategists & visionaries.
   b. Their jobs are very secure.
   c. They're "big picture" people.

3. Getting a respected member of top management to sponsor your business plan can help you communicate and get approval for your plan.   ❑ True   ❑ False

4. When meeting to propose the business plan, it's important to keep the meeting as short as possible while presenting all the key data.   ❑ True   ❑ False

5. Questions from the executives during the presentation meeting are a sign of disrespect and aggression.   ❑ True   ❑ False

Answer key: 1. f; 2. b; 3. T; 4. T; 5. F

Strategic staffing

Ivan is the HR director at a large consumer research company whose primary source of revenue stems from quarterly reports of consumer purchasing behavior. The raw data for the reports is collected over a period of six weeks through numerous and extensive consumer interviews, the results of which are then run through sophisticated statistical analysis software programs. The company supplements its revenue stream by conducting smaller, customized studies when they are not processing the quarterly reports. Ivan needs to come up with a staffing plan. Where does he begin?

Refocus perceptions

Staffing is the grand dame of HR functions; everyone knows that HR "does staffing." The trouble is, many also see the function solely as necessary overhead. So how can you take it to the next level? How can you change the perception of the staffing function, demonstrate that strategic staffing can provide value to the business, and get others to recognize it as the crown jewel that it can be?

It all starts with the business. Be proactive. Know your company's business objectives and frame your staffing solutions in terms of how they can help your company meet those objectives.

Are your staffing efforts driven only by head count and focused on bringing in more bodies? Do they lack a focused direction? If so, it may be time to align your staffing plan with your company's business strategy. A proactive strategic staffing plan that is in alignment with the company's business objectives can provide your company with the talent that will give it a competitive edge. Strive for synergy between the staffing function and organizational objectives.

Dr. John Sullivan, in "Selecting Your Employment Strategy" (*www.drjohnsullivan.com*, February 26, 1999), maintains that successful staffing strategies share the following traits:

- ◆ They are aligned with the company's business strategy and provide it with a competitive advantage.
- ◆ They fit the environment in which the company operates.
- ◆ Both attraction and retention components are included.
- ◆ The strategy is communicated and understood.
- ◆ Metrics measure whether or not the strategy is achieving its goals.

Making the connection: A case study on retention

Well structured incentive programs are a great way to connect business objectives with staffing strategies. Consider the case of Dawson Personnel Systems in Columbus, Ohio. Vice president and partner David DeCapua wanted to retain talented, high-performing employees. Being in the staffing business, Dawson's employees were talking to other companies all day long. DeCapua would hear employees say things like "ABC company allows its employees to take off on their birthdays, or that another closes down for a company outing."

Bankers' hours. What DeCapua came up with was extra paid time off if certain productivity goals are met. "I don't know whoever said that you have to work 40 hours a week," he says. "The real truth is that you're lucky if you get 40 percent or 50 percent productivity in 40 hours. We began to wonder whether, by scaling back the hours, we could get 100 percent out of our employees. And, that's exactly what happened."

Offered first to DeCapua's sales staff, the program allows a salesperson to work "bankers' hours" for the rest of the month as soon as that individual's monthly sales goal is met. This means, for example, that if an employee reaches his sales goal on the third day of the month, he can work from 8:30 a.m. to 2 p.m. for the rest of the month. In addition, if that salesperson also happens to be the first person to reach the goal that month, he receives an additional two days off at the end of the month.

Goal setting. Setting the goal for sales staff is easy, admits DeCapua. "Ask yourself: 'In my business, what would be considered a really big month for a salesperson?' Then, raise the bar 20 percent." But he found that setting goals and structuring the rewards for employees in his administrative and accounting departments was much harder.

"I deferred to my department managers," he says. In turn, the managers polled employees and asked how such a program could work for them. According to DeCapua, some employees asked for Mondays or Fridays off. "I told them that if you can get your work done in a four-day time frame, that's fine. But, you have to include everybody in your program," DeCapua says. "Sometimes, companies offer these incentives only for sales staff and that's not fair."

If there is one hitch, it's the fact that employees are expected to check in for messages during their time away from the office. Cell phones and e-mail make that easy.

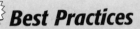

Best Practices

Same day hiring has its rewards

An incentive program for recruiters was implemented at Superior Bank to convey the message to its hiring managers and recruiters that if "you snooze, you loose." Recruiters are awarded points toward merchant catalog gifts for every candidate that is closed in a single day's turnaround. Turnaround is defined as: an interview with the hiring manager, a discussion of the candidate's qualifications with the recruiter, a recommendation and approval on the hiring rate, a phone call and an acceptance by the candidate.

—Peter Altuch, Superior Bank, from "Sharing Best Practices In Recruiting" by Dr. John Sullivan, www.drjohnsullivan.com (November 12, 1999).

Finding the right strategy

Staffing strategies define where a company focuses its human capital and priorities. Optimal results are achieved when the staffing and business strategies are in alignment. After all, a "well-oiled staffing machine" that consistently brings in just "average" employees at a fantastic cost per hire will do little to help a company that strives to be the most innovative in its field.

Position analysis

So how do you develop a strategic staffing plan? Once you've identified your company's goals and objectives, analyze each position:

- ◆ What is the business justification for the position?
- ◆ How does the position contribute to the company's goals?
- ◆ What behaviors are necessary to fulfill the position's objectives?
- ◆ What unique characteristics or specific problems exist in your work force?

Example: *The position of buyer for a retail chain requires that the employee have knowledge of the purchasing process, how to negotiate the best value for the dollars spent and how to manage inventory against an "open to buy" budget. But very* *different candidates would be sought after depending on the retailer's market strategy: a mass merchant discounter would look for a buyer who understands price sensitivity, whereas an up-scale boutique would look for a buyer with an eye for fashion and trends.*

Each level within an organization may also require a different strategy. If, for example, your company needs a lot of people with adequate data entry skills, your strategy may be to bring in average performers at average pay. But when it comes time to bring in that special VP who can convey the company's vision and energize the work force, average will not be "good enough."

The strategy behind selecting the right combination of skills, experience and knowledge is driven by the business objectives of the organization, and the recruitment methods are, in turn, driven by what you're looking for in an employee. While temporary-to-permanent may be the way to go for the data entry positions, a "headhunter" or executive search firm may be a better approach to finding that special VP.

WHAT you need to know

Staffing levels

Also examine workload and job interdependencies. Identify peak workload periods involving an influx of outside calls, person-to-person contact with the public and e-mail or other technical interfaces. Identify interdependency among sections or individual employees. Anticipate staffing growth and reductions.

Example: *ABC Company manufactures space heaters all year long. As inventory is completed, it is either shipped to customers or sent to ABC Company's warehouse for later delivery. While the assembly line runs at full capacity all year long, 80 percent of ABC Company's customers want delivery of space heaters in the fall and winter months, necessitating seasonal adjustments in the staffing levels of the shipping and warehouse departments.*

Hiring environment

HR professionals know all too well that any staffing strategy must recognize the realities of the marketplace and how the economy, both national and global, impacts their business. Is the economy weak and the unemployment rate high? If so, you'll likely have a good selection of highly qualified and skilled candidates. If not, you may be faced with a war for talent and your ability to attract and retain the candidates of your choice could be a real challenge.

Geography, too, plays a role. What does the applicant pool look like? Where do your potential candidates live? Is there a transportation network in place that will allow you to hire the workers that you need? For example, if your company is located near a university you may have an abundant supply of students who are seeking part-time work. If you're in a suburban location and you're looking for minority candidates from the inner city, will you need to supplement public transportation by providing shuttle service from your company to the train or bus depot?

Employer culture

Work environment and benefits. Employer culture plays an important role in selecting a staffing strategy. Both an appealing work environment and an attractive benefit package are powerful drivers in attracting and retaining the right employees. Work environment and generous benefits are often part of a company's staffing strategy. Progressive personnel policies are a starting point for creating a public perception that a company is a good place to work.

DON'T miss this

If you know the hiring manager's likes and dislikes, you'll have a better chance of sending her candidates who are a good fit for that position. One strategy might involve interviewing the person you're hiring for—find out who's been successful in her department and who has not, who has stayed and who was let go, who's considered a favorite and who is not. Or consider using exit interviews to support strategy in hiring new people. Say, for example, you find out everyone's leaving one manager because he's constantly screaming. Depending on the circumstances, you may want to counsel him, or you may want to make sure that new hires are thick-skinned and forewarned.

Employer of choice. Significant recruiting value can result from being considered an "employer of choice." Companies report that, due in part to their reputations as being among *Fortune* magazine's most admired companies, applications for positions constantly are submitted without solicitation.

Valued employees. A company that understands the critical contribution people make to the bottom line and establishes an atmosphere and culture that allows people to make their greatest possible contribution will often find recruiting easier.

Employees also value a "clear sense of organizational purpose" to a great extent, so much so that it influences their choice of an employer.

✓ *Checklist*

Policy areas that impact recruiting effort

Following are some of the policy areas that can impact recruiting practices and, in addition, can affect an organization's status as an employer of choice:

- ☐ **EEO.** Affirmative action programs may require hiring of minorities or development of minorities to fill certain positions. Federal contractors must meet hiring guidelines.
- ☐ **Compensation.** Management may want to position its pay ranges to attract the top performers from other companies or may decide to set salaries at the median for the market, depending upon its strategy.
- ☐ **Succession planning.** The need for depth at certain positions may mandate recruiting in different ways.
- ☐ **Labor relations.** A management commitment to stay union-free may affect hiring practices or the areas from which the company recruits.
- ☐ **Skills requirements.** Are training programs in place to teach employees needed workplace skills or specific job skills, or must management recruit workers who are already capable of performing job tasks?

Continued on next page

Continued from previous page

☐ **Diverse work force.** Different recruiting methods may be needed to attract women, older workers and minorities that make up an increasingly larger part of the available labor force.

☐ **Company culture.** Does the corporate culture require a specific personality type? Are there barriers to recruiting that originate in the public perception of the company?

☐ **Headcount and staffing policies.** Whether the company uses job rotation and promotion from within or hiring from outside to fill job vacancies can determine the frequency and type of recruitment for certain job titles.

☐ **Recruiting targets**. Is there a commitment to recruit from specific colleges or schools? Is there a commitment to hire from minority colleges? Does management prefer to hire new graduates or experienced professionals? How do these choices impact the overall business strategy?

☐ **Benefits package.** Does the benefits package offer a variety of benefits that appeal to all segments of the work force? Is the package competitive? Are benefits discussed early in the recruiting process? Employees have indicated that 401(k) retirement or savings plans, along with pension plans and medical insurance, would significantly influence their choice of an employer.

Ideas from the front lines

Wondering what some companies are doing in terms of staffing strategies? Take a look at some of the best practice strategies that real HR professionals have tried and liked.

DON'T miss this

Always remember that "strategic" staffing isn't just about having good staffing strategies; it's really all about aligning those staffing approaches with the organization's business purposes.

Best Practices

Ideas from the front lines

Sell your company. If you want to get top recruits, you must begin selling your company even before you start recruiting. For example, make investor reports available and have a web site. Once you get the recruits in, you must move quickly or you will lose them to another company. Continue to sell the company by telling them about company plans and strategies. Help them meet people. Talk to them about coming to your company and making a difference.

—Alicia Whitaker, Executive Director, Strategic Staffing and Organization Development, Pitney-Bowes, Inc. speaking at The Conference Board's 1999 Human Resources Conference.

Continental promotes itself as a "great place to work" and emphasizes the perks of working in the airline industry, such as free trips and buddy passes to take friends along. We want team players. Now people want to be associated with the company. Success builds success. Company officers meet with recruits to connect them right up with the company culture.

—Michael Campbell, Senior Vice President of Human Resources and Labor Relations, Continental Airlines, Inc. speaking at The Conference Board's 1999 Human Resources Conference.

Debrief new people. We are always looking for ways to find the "passive job seeker," the person who is not actively looking but could be interested in a new job. When we bring in new senior people, we debrief them on the best talent they know. We are working on putting that information in a database.

—Alicia Whitaker, Executive Director, Strategic Staffing and Organization Development, Pitney-Bowes, Inc. speaking at The Conference Board's 1999 Human Resources Conference.

Best Practices

Pitch potential and the future. At Kodak, our challenges are bringing the company into the digital world. Managers act as recruiters, finding new talent as they network. We make managers aware of this expectation and highlight role models who have brought in great talent. We help to identify forums for the managers, but do not really provide training on this. We also use outside recruiters for certain capabilities. The Kodak brand is prominent, and consumer photography is growing.

—Robert L. Berman, Director of Human Resources and Vice President, Consumer Imaging, Eastman Kodak Company speaking at The Conference Board's 1999 Human Resources Conference.

Mine references. Checking references can turn into a two-for-one deal. Janelle Everett uses the chore of reference checking as a way to market her company. It takes an extra 10 to 12 minutes but presents the opportunity for great returns. "If we found a second candidate 1 in 15 times this way, we could improve our recruiting efforts by 6 percent—with no additional costs and minimal time on the part of HR. If nothing else comes out of it, we have improved our brand image, and what's that worth?"

—Janelle Everett, Mulberry Neckwear, from "Sharing Best Practices In Recruiting" by Dr. John Sullivan, www.drjohnsullivan.com (November 12, 1999).

Mike Walton looks at the job titles in the reference section of resumes. If he needs a General Manager, he looks for GM references and gives them a call to find out if they know of a good GM candidate for his open position.

—Mike Walton, MCI Worldcom, from "Sharing Best Practices In Recruiting" by Dr. John Sullivan, www.drjohnsullivan.com (November 12, 1999).

A⁺ *Best Practices*

Online newsletters. E-news distribution lists tend to be more up-to-date than traditional mailing lists.

If you find that your contact database is dated, consider purchasing the distribution lists for electronic newsletters that relate to your company's market or that your company's top performers subscribe to. Another option would be to sponsor a contest through an online newsletter. That approach would allow you to pre-screen candidates and collect contact information.

—Dr. John Sullivan and Master Burnett in "Rebuilding Your Staffing Function: It's Past Time To Get Started," www.drjohnsullivan.com (July 1, 2002).

Help finding the next job. The Chicago Panel, a nonprofit organization with a mission to improve schools and education for Chicago's children, deals with budget and staffing challenges by focusing on non-cash elements to attract and retain part-time employees and consultants. While with the Panel, employees would be given opportunities to gain experience they might not have otherwise gotten until later in their careers—project development and management, attribution and acknowledgement in Panel publications and networking and speaking opportunities.

But it is recognized that most employees will stay with the Panel only one or two years. When employees begin their hunt for a new job, the Panel's Executive Director actively works to connect them to her network of contacts and provides advice and guidance. Employees, in exchange, commit to finishing their projects and to help find and train their replacements.

—The Chicago Area Partnership, "Pathways and Progress: Best Practices to Ensure Fair Compensation," May 2003. The report is available at www.womenemployed.org.

✓ Checklist

Staffing strategies

Company philosophies, operations and values vary considerably. Yet these are the drivers behind their staffing strategies. To have your staffing strategy support your company's needs, you need first to know and understand your business—and what kind of employees it needs to succeed. After you've determined that, take a look at this sampling of potential strategies:

☐ Target the best and the brightest.
☐ Target high-profile individuals.
☐ Target individuals "with connections."
☐ Target employee referrals.
☐ Target new college graduates.
☐ Target active job seekers.
☐ Target passive job seekers.
☐ Target techno-savy, web surfers.
☐ Target priority positions.
☐ Target entry-level positions.
☐ Target skills.
☐ Target competencies.
☐ Target experience.
☐ Target attitude.
☐ Target diversity.
☐ Raid the competition.
☐ Fill open requisitions only.
☐ Maintain continuous relationships.
☐ Become an employer of choice.
☐ Align recruiting with marketing.
☐ Promote from within.
☐ Hire permanent employees only from your temporary work force.
☐ Acquire talent through mergers and acquisitions.
☐ Hire fast.
☐ Take your time and find the right person.

Reevaluate your plan

Strategic staffing never ends. Just as your company's business plan continues to evolve with time to meet the demands of market forces and new challenges, so should a strategic staffing plan.

Measure how well your plan is doing. The staffing function can be measured in a number of ways: cost per hire, number of hires, speed of hire, satisfaction of hire and quality of hire. Although harder to measure, quality of hire is perhaps the most strategic way to measure the success of a staffing plan. A high return on investment is much more desirable than a low cost per hire.

Look at the plan as it exists today and make projections for three and five years out. Then continually reevaluate the plan to see if it's on target and especially if the target has moved. With the amount of organizational change now taking place, it's imperative to continue to reevaluate how aligned your staffing approach is with your organizational objectives.

The right mix: Staffing alternatives

Internal options

Regular, full-time employees form the core of most, but not all, organizations' work forces. They generally work 40 or more hours per week and are entitled to benefits. Because regular, full-time employees are expensive, a strategic staffing plan will pay close attention to appropriate staffing levels of regular, full-time employees.

Many organizations utilize existing staff in nontraditional ways to achieve more productive results. These methods modify the ways in which positions are staffed and include:

- ◆ Part-time employees;
- ◆ Internal temporary staff pools;
- ◆ On-call emergency staff pools;
- ◆ Increasing overtime hours;
- ◆ Flextime scheduling;
- ◆ Job sharing; and
- ◆ Telecommuting.

Whether or not various internal staffing methods are appropriate for a business depends upon:

◆ The demands of the work;
◆ Marketplace constraints;
◆ Costs; and
◆ Customer service considerations.

Example: *A fast food restaurant needs more workers during the busy lunch and dinner hours and fewer workers between meal times. It may be more cost-effective to staff it with a full-time manager and multiple part-time workers than to have a crew of regular full-time employees.*

Similarly, a specialty gift store may need to bring in more workers at Christmastime than at other times of the year. Yet at that time of year, given the loyal clientele, it's critical to have knowledgeable workers who can provide a high level of service. Typical "temps" who lack specialized experience may not be appropriate. However, hiring retirees who are also loyal customers and who have proven knowledgeable about the merchandise to work during the holiday period may solve the workload issue and increase customer satisfaction.

External options

Companies have long used temporary or contingent labor to fill in when regular employees are absent or to perform specialized projects. Over the past decade, the use of contingent or supplemental staffing has incresed substantially for a number of reasons, including a need to:

◆ Retain flexibility in size due to an uncertain economy or following downsizing or reengineering.
◆ Accommodate lifestyle pressures of individuals for part-time or flex-place work.
◆ Easily integrate new work methods and practices.
◆ Add staff without retraining to adjust to a rapidly changing technology.
◆ Transfer responsibility to perform or provide non-core functions and concentrate on core functions of business.
◆ Control the rising cost of employee benefits or overtime.

Temporary workers. Temporary help is a long-standing concept that traditionally provided temporary or fill-in help through an outside agency. It's evolved to the point at which, in 1997, ManPower was the largest private employer in the country. And the concept is no longer confined to office help—temporary physicists, lawyers or chemists are now available. There are also a growing number of international linkages.

WHAT you need to know

Temporary staffing companies recruit, train and pay their employees, who then fill in for a "client" employer on a temporary basis. On the other hand, a professional employer organization (PEO) is a company that arranges to shift the client company's permanent employees onto its own payroll. The PEO handles all the administrative functions while the client company handles day-to-day operations. The PEO in effect becomes the HR specialist.

The reasons for using a temp agency or a PEO differ. With temporary agencies, the client employer may need help on a one-time project, or may have a hard time attracting new employees in a tough labor market. Many employers use temporary agencies as screening devices to weed out poor performers. With PEOs, employers are primarily looking to shift the burden of handling administrative issues.

Leased employees. Employee leasing is a term that can mean different things in different circumstances; however, it generally refers to a situation in which a company "employs" the staff of an employer and bills the employer for expenses and a fee for management services. The employer hires the firm to find qualified employees, assume various administrative burdens associated with personnel administration and, perhaps, to provide additional benefits to employees. Leased workers tend to come on board for a particular employer for a longer period of time than temporary employees—generally for the duration of a project.

Any leasing agreement should be made with a clear understanding of the employer's potential legal liabilities. It's not always clear who the employer is and who assumes the responsibilities and risks of the employment relationship. These issues are particularly important because subscribers to leasing services may remain legally accountable for their employees in various ways, such as employee lawsuits, workers' compensation claims, wage-hour violations and benefits obligations.

Contract workers. This arrangement does not make use of an outside agency. Contract workers may be difficult to distinguish from an employer's regular work force and are often former employees who return for less money, fewer or no benefits and no job security.

✓ Checklist

Factors to consider before hiring a staffing company

Contracting with an agency to provide individuals or services is like negotiating any important contract. Companies should seek legal guidance to be properly protected. Among other things, consideration should be given to:

☐ Clearly designating the responsibilities and services of each party—hiring, firing, training, assigning work, making work rules, etc.

☐ Carefully drafting hold harmless and indemnification clauses.

☐ Specifying job descriptions.

☐ Indicating situations that may cause the parties to terminate or cancel the contract.

☐ Delineating any confidentiality requirements.

☐ Covering issues such as termination policies in the event of poor performance, prompt payment and grace period, or penalties for failing to comply with contract terms.

☐ Stipulating which party is responsible for payroll, withholding and payment of use, excise, value added or similar taxes for the individuals.

☐ Clarifying who has primary responsibility for paying and providing workers' compensation insurance and who has the immunity protection.

☐ Indicating which entity will provide employee benefits, if any, and if the staffing company must make a contribution to the benefits offered.

Think back to the beginning of the chapter when we discussed Ivan, the HR director looking to create a staffing plan for a consumer research company with intermittent staffing needs. The right staffing mix will be essential if Ivan wants to step up to the table and become a strategic partner who can help his company achieve their business objectives.

Know the business objectives. One of the first things Ivan needs to know is what those business objectives are. Ivan's plan will look different if his company is focused on long-term, stable profitability, or the "here and now" to enhance its appearance with the investment community or to be seen as an attractive target for acquisition.

Analyze the position. Ivan will want to look at the research interviewer position very closely. What skills are required, and are these skills that employees bring with them? Or must they be taught? Perhaps Ivan can use temporary employees who possess good communication skills. Is any specialized training necessary to conduct study interviews? Does each study require an orientation, or is generalized training sufficient to conduct all study interviews? If specialized training is required, Ivan might want to look at using his own employees (either full-time or part-time) rather than temporary workers.

Analyze the project impact of your staffing approach. Assuming that each study needs specialized orientation training, Ivan must look at the right mix of full-time and part-time employees. Unlike part-time employees who forget the specifics of a study from quarter to quarter, full-time employees would have the opportunity to practice their skills and would not need orientation training each quarter. But is it profitable to keep them on the payroll during "down times" when no work is available? Maybe not in the short term. But would full-timers' increased effectiveness and reduced need for training make them the more profitable alternative in the long run?

Staffing strategies for "hot" jobs

IS/IT workers look for advancement

The median voluntary turnover rate for information systems/information technology (IS/IT) employees dropped a percentage point in 2003 (4 percent compared to 5 percent in 2002). Nevertheless, employers could be at risk of losing their high-performing IT workers if they don't keep them happy. And that seems to mean a clear path to advancement. According to Hewitt Associates "2003 U.S. HOT Technologies Survey," the number one reason that IS/IT workers leave a company is for promotion to a higher-level job (cited by 42 percent of the responding companies). They also leave for a chance to learn the latest technology (10 percent) and a lack of a defined career path (8 percent).

Once they're gone, employers will need to compete for a replacement. According to the Hewitt study, the most common recruiting sources for hot-skill IT candidates are:

- ◆ Employee referrals and Internet recruiting (tied for first place with 96 percent each);
- ◆ Internal transfers (78 percent); and
- ◆ Search firms (64 percent).

Regarding the effectiveness of the recruiting sources, the study found:

- ◆ 23 percent of IS/IT hires came from internal recruiters;
- ◆ 20 percent came from the Internet;
- ◆ 17 percent from employee referrals; and
- ◆ 16 percent from internal transfer.

DON'T miss this

How critical is IT to your organization's success? Are your business strategies highly dependent on the latest technology? Are competitors making inroads in your markets based on leveraging technological advances? If these factors are true for your company, for strategic attraction and retention make sure your staffing strategies for IS/IT personnel include fast-track advancement opportunities, cutting edge technical training and a clear career path.

Nurses look for working conditions, respect

In "An Acute Condition: Too Few Nurses" (*HR Magazine*, December 2002) author Diane Cadrain examines why a nursing shortage exists and what employers can do to deal with it. The dominant themes are recruitment that appeals to the nurses' quality of work life, focused retention efforts and getting more nurses in the educational pipeline.

Temporary and foreign nurses are one option for dealing with the shortage, but they can be expensive and take time away from staff nurses while learning a new culture. By supporting the features that make temp work an attractive option for nurses, says the American Nursing Association's president Barbara Blakeney, hospitals can better retain their regular staff. A culture of retention entails promoting teamwork, creating a positive nursing environment by lowering patient-nurse ratios, giving nurses more decision-making authority, letting nurses have a say in setting appropriate work levels, and reducing mandatory overtime.

Dr. Nancy Woods, dean of the University of Washington School of Nursing, says that hospitals with the best retention rates allow nurses to give patients the level of care that they want to deliver. She points to the concept of magnet hospitals for fostering empowerment of, and respect for, nurses. A subsidiary of the American Nursing Association, the American Nurses Credentialing Center recognizes health care organizations that provide the best nursing care.

With the shortage of nurses projected to continue at an alarming rate (275,000 by 2010, to 507,000 by 2015, and to 808,000 by 2020), many in the field stress the need to work with educational facilities. Lisa Helle of Montana Hospital Association Ventures Inc. suggests that hospitals get out the word to teachers and counselors and make hospitals open to visits from interested students. Anthony Disser, chief nurse executive at Inova Fairfax Hospital, suggests summer externship programs that allow nursing students to work during college breaks and position them for first choice of jobs when they graduate.

**WHAT
you need
to know**

Which of these recruiting and staffing strategies best aligns with your organizational realities? Perhaps your organization is in a posture requiring substantial cost-cutting measures, as is true throughout many segments of the healthcare industry. Which of the strategies above could foster more autonomy among nurses and yet still reduce costs? Have you considered involving your top nurses in devising such a strategy? Or have you been able to make the business case that improved retention will in fact reduce costs enough to allow nurses more of a say in staffing levels?

A+ *Best Practices*

Elitism in the mortgage lending business

Mortgage lenders have had a hard time finding qualified people in the early part of the 21st century. So much so that many employers are satisfied just to meet their numbers. But HomeBanc's Chief People Officer Dwight Reighard wanted more. He wanted employees with a strong value system—employees who were involved in service to their communities and who would buy into a "service-leadership" model.

His strategy. Reighard modeled a campaign on that of the U.S. Marines. Author Eilene Zimmerman describes Reighard's strategy in "The Patriotic Recruiting Gospel of a Chief People Officer" (Workforce Online, July 2003). Launched in early March 2003, the campaign combines patriotic general branding ads with recruitment advertising that asks candidates if they've "got what it takes." The ads use terms like "service oriented," "dedication" and "loyalty."

Initial results are promising. HomeBanc had 400 online applications in February 2003 without advertising, a number that jumped to 1,203 in March 2003 and hit 1,551 in June 2003. And there's the added benefit of letting potential customers know that HomeBanc hires only the best.

This is an excellent example of dovetailing your staffing strategy with your marketing strategy, especially in an industry that is dependent upon service.

Diversity

Traditionally, the HR staffing function looked at work force composition in terms of legal compliance—how to ensure that staffing decisions were not discriminatory on the basis of race, sex, religion, age, national origin or other protected traits. Strategic staffing knows that there are competitive advantages to work force diversity and capitalizes on those advantages.

> Recruiting should be planned so that it uses sources and methods likely to reach a diverse audience, including women and minorities. Use of methods that produce only a narrow selection of applicants—relying heavily on the referrals from a white, male work force, for instance—is likely to be found to be discriminatory and illegal.

WHAT you need to know

The realities of America's shifting demographics are causing companies to rethink the way they hire, promote and retain employees. It's as much a bottom line issue as it is a matter of evaluating new points of view. The business case for diversity in the workplace is simple: It can lead to increased revenues and profits.

In short, diversity drives employee satisfaction, which drives customer satisfaction, which drives profits that can be measured in terms of customer retention, repeat sales and referrals. Diversity also creates a richer work environment, with improved decision-making, because opinions are drawn from a wider variety of viewpoints.

DON'T miss this

According to a 2001 survey by the Society for Human Resource Management (SHRM) and *Fortune* magazine, 91 percent of the HR professionals credited diversity initiatives with helping maintain a competitive edge. Improvements cited in the SHRM/*Fortune* "Impact of Diversity Initiatives on Bottom Line Survey" ranged from enhancing the corporate culture to bettering client relations:

Benefits of diversity initiatives

improved corporate culture	79%
improved recruitment of new employees	77%
improved client relationships	52%
higher employee retention	41%

On which aspects of diversity are organizations focusing? The following graph shows what respondents said their diversity efforts include:

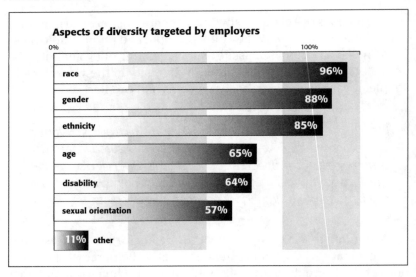

Aspects of diversity targeted by employers

race	96%
gender	88%
ethnicity	85%
age	65%
disability	64%
sexual orientation	57%
other	11%

"Other" aspects of diversity include thinking styles and patterns, marital status, seniority, education, socio-economic status, merging company cultures and management and union relationships.

While most companies succeed at recruiting diverse talent, they are not as successful in diversifying senior levels. "You must look at every layer of organization," says Jose Berrios, Vice President of Staffing and Diversity for the Gannett Company. You must also look beyond gender and race. For example, in traditional areas such as publishing, gay and lesbian representation is a "tough nut to crack." To try to break this barrier, Gannett (a publishing company) implemented same-sex partner benefits.

Internet and technology solutions

New technologies are making it easier for employers to locate job seekers and process the thousands of resumes received each year. Online recruiting takes advantage of the tremendous growth of the World Wide Web, and the Internet offers sites on which employers can post job openings and/or view the resumes of job seekers.

Specialized software services have developed that allow employers to digitize resumes, deposit them in databases and match up job requirements with candidates' skills and competencies. Some companies even offer their services to job seekers who want to put their resumes into electronic scannable format to better increase their chances of finding employment.

Certainly the new technology can represent a great savings in terms of the time and dollars involved in processing and reviewing resumes. It has the added advantages of being able to target a specific type of candidate and to generate wide exposure.

Online recruiting can magnify the problem of tracking applicant flow data because the necessary information on race and gender may not be available to the employer, particularly if the job bank or database is created by someone other than the employer.

When using electronic databases, be sure to select those that have the capability of maintaining applicant-flow data by protected status and can provide you with the information necessary for EEO compliance.

✓ Checklist

What to look for in job-posting web sites

HR professionals looking to use the Internet to recruit new employees need to view job-posting websites through the eyes of a job hunter, says Jane M. Lommel of the Hudson Institute. That approach will help them to assess whether the sites will effectively attract job candidates. HR pros would be well-advised to post their job openings on web sites that score high on the following elements.

☐ **Speed.** E-ads have great potential, but job hunters using the Internet are likely to have a short attention span. Speed is really, really critical. Potential candidates can lose interest in web sites with pages that take more than three seconds to download.

☐ **Good design elements.** Effective web sites are likely to have a savvy, friendly design. Attractive pages can make a positive first impression. Similarly, good web sites are easy to navigate, with a simple and logical flow from page to page. Complex pages are a turnoff to job hunters.

☐ **Interactivity.** Many job seekers appreciate web sites with useful interactive features, such as the ability to electronically submit resumes or receive e-mail about new job postings. Again, these features should be simple and easy to use.

☐ **Content.** Another attribute of a good job web site is creative and appropriate content. Appropriate content, for instance, may include salary information or details about the community where a job is located.

Best Practices

Online behavioral interview finds talent fast

With a long-term business model calling for 10 to 12 percent annual growth in new restaurants, Chili's VP Jan Barr knew that finding enough management talent would be key to the initiative's success. Chili's was getting as many as 1,500 electronic resumes a week, but without an online screening tool it was taking a recruiter one full day per week just to open and glance at the resumes. Recruiters were interviewing 10 to 12 candidates a day and were traveling 50 to 70 percent of the month, but were hiring on average only one in 12 restaurant-management candidates.

In "Chili's Hot Interview Makeover" (Workforce Online, July 2003), author Rachael King explains how Chili's brought the number of candidates hired up to one in seven by implementing an online behavioral interview system. Barr and her team worked with Behavior Description Technologies to adjust its "e.ssessor" online interview program to meet Chili's needs.

Along with basic information (contact information, work history, education, salary expectations, etc.), candidates were asked to answer behavioral interview questions about their past performance and how they've met challenges. With the preliminary screening done up front, recruiters don't waste time, and follow-up interviews are more focused.

The system reached ROI in the first six months because recruiters now spend only three to five percent of their time traveling. And the interview-to-hire ratio has gone to one in seven. In fact, the system has saved so much time that Chili's no longer needs full-time recruiters, and they are now training to become HR managers.

Succession planning

Truly strategic staffing plans will have succession planning as one of their elements. Succession planning is a process that results in a formal business plan. This plan identifies talent (existing staff or profiles of recruitment needs) for key managerial/leadership roles in the organization in the future. The objective of succession planning is to ensure that the organization (or a unit of the organization) will continue to be effective and competitive.

Succession planning should include all positions that are critical to the company's future. Thus a succession plan may not include all existing managerial positions and may include positions that will never be supervisory or managerial. To be effective, succession planning must identify those positions that represent critical elements of the organization's business strategy and then align the skills and abilities integral to those positions with that strategy.

Example: In many organizations, technology staff is critical to on-going production and to complete new initiatives. In other organizations, members of the sales or customer service staff may be critical because of relationships developed over many years. And for some organizations, there may be employees such as the Corporate Secretary whose institutional memory is essential to several key tasks.

Conversely, there may be managers who hold their positions based primarily on seniority, status quo and the personality of the incumbent. In the event the position becomes vacant, the position would not be filled at the same managerial level, assuming that it is filled at all.

What it's not

Succession planning is not:

◆ A technique to plan individual career advancement opportunities;

◆ A reward for high performers; or

◆ Replacement hiring, which assumes that since the position is open, it should be filled with a candidate (internal or external) that reflects the abilities of the former incumbent or the job criteria as currently described.

✓ *Checklist*

Reasons for succession planning

☐ **Survival.** For many, if not all, businesses survival depends upon the caliber of decision-making and knowledge of the talent in key roles. Succession planning ensures that key talent will be available.

☐ **New and increasing business risks.** Downsizing, management turnover, diminishing job security, process re-engineering, employee empowerment initiatives, financial pressures to "do more with less," and lack of belief in long-term career growth are some risks that impact on the retention of key talent. These pressures contribute to the importance of management succession planning.

☐ **Diminishing talent pool.** As a general rule in stable businesses, the number of mid-management positions have been reduced which, in turn, reduces the pool of promotable talent for upper or executive management positions. As a group, mid-level managers reflect diminishing morale. Competition is increasing globally, and executive positions are requiring greater risk-taking, knowledge and technology. These trends also contribute to the value of effective succession planning.

☐ **Force change.** Typically, if not planned but instead left to chance, talent will not be available when an organization needs it, and instead managers will continue to promote individuals that, as a general rule, are similar to themselves.

☐ **Risk avoidance.** Tragedy can strike a company. Failure to plan can leave a vacuum in leadership from which a company cannot recover.

Don't make the mistake of thinking that you have a "strategic staffing plan" just because you have a succession plan in place. It is important to remember that succession planning is only one component; a strategic staffing plan must align today's staffing needs and business objectives, as well as plan for future needs. And, of course, a strategic staffing plan must be integrated with employee development plans and reward and recognition systems.

Tell or not to tell?

Should an employer tell employees whether or not they are included in the company's succession plan? Which approach best meets the strategic business objectives of your organization? Arguments include:

◆ Judgments about a person's potential are very subjective. There may be contingencies that will change the decision when an opening actually occurs. An employee may perceive that the position was "promised" to them, thus resulting in protracted litigation.

◆ Key employees may leave a company because they didn't feel they had greater career potential. Money and time invested in those employees can be wasted.

Whatever the organization decides, the decision must be communicated to avoid the situation in which one manager will tell and another will not. One approach is to consider telling employees that they're going to be provided additional developmental opportunities and training without identifying a specific position.

Obstacles to succession planning

Succession planning must be done in concert with strategic planning and can provide a basis for enhancing managerial training programs. Yet most businesses struggle with the task of succession planning because of factors including:

◆ Reduction of management levels within an organization;

◆ Downsizing or re-engineering in the company or in the industry;

◆ Turnover at the entry and middle management levels;

◆ Technology changes; and

◆ Competitive pressures.

The Quiz

1. Strategic staffing requires that staffing policies be integrated with other company policies. ❑ True ❑ False

2. Which of the following is not an element of a successful staffing strategy?
   a. Alignment with business strategy.
   b. Fit with the environment in which the company operates.
   c. Attraction component.
   d. Retention component.
   e. Facility security.
   f. Communication.
   g. Measured results.

3. Strategic staffing requires an analysis of:
   a. Positions.
   b. Company culture.
   c. Business objectives.
   d. Hiring environment.
   e. All of the above.
   f. All except c.

4. The reasons for using a temp agency or a professional employer organization differ. ❑ True ❑ False

5. Cost per hire is always the best method of measuring staffing success. ❑ True ❑ False

6. Succession planning should include all positions within the company. ❑ True ❑ False

Answer key: 1. T; 2. e; 3. e; 4. T; 5. F; 6. F

Strategic compensation

Carlos is the HR director at a high-tech fiber optics company. The company's highly competitive environment demands that it stay on the cutting edge of research and new product development. The information technology (IT) department has been working with several contractors to help with systems that support these new product development functions, and two people, Anthony and LaDonna, have proven particularly skilled. One particular IT project is vital to the company's new product launch, and LaDonna says she can get that project done in two weeks. The IT Director, Lionel, wants to hire both consultants as permanent employees. As consultants, Anthony made $50 per hour and LaDonna made $40 per hour. Lionel wonders if their talent is worth hiring them at salaries equivalent to their consultant fees. How would it be justified? What would their total compensation packages be worth? Would they help meet the company's strategic objectives?

What is strategic compensation?

Being strategic in HR means getting the right people in the right place for the right price at the right time. Strategic compensation is an *investment* to get the desired behaviors and results from your employees. Compensation is defined by WorldatWork as the elements of pay (base, variable, stock, etc.) that an employer offers an employee in return for services rendered to the employer. For the employer, compensation can be defined as the cost of providing those economic benefits to the employee.

WHAT you need to know

> Effective compensation strategies are critical because they are the primary means for attracting, retaining and motivating talented employees. Organizations need the mission to achieve strategic organization objectives.

Strategic total compensation packages should be developed to fit the organization's needs and include base pay structures, alternative or flexible pay systems and variable programs. In addition, total compensation packages include components such as:

◆ Work environment;
◆ Opportunity for advancement;
◆ Health benefits;
◆ Corporate culture;
◆ Work style flexibility;
◆ Retirement benefits;
◆ Paid time off;
◆ Casual dress code; and
◆ Work/life benefits.

Compensation strategies must help the company achieve its strategic business goals and mission. Keep in mind that what works well in one company might not work well in another. Management must ensure that compensation programs are consistent with the goals and personality of the employer.

Example: *Consider a sporting goods retailer whose objective is to "supply customers with sports equipment and supplies that fit their personalities, interests and incomes while enhancing their enjoyment of physical fitness and competition." This objective focuses the resources and attention of the retailing company on meeting customer needs, encouraging fitness and competition and enhancing its customers' leisure time.*

A strategic compensation strategy needs to support and contribute to achieving this objective and align employee interests with that objective. That strategy might design pay programs in a way that encourages competency in key skill areas, such as personal wellness, industry expertise and sales techniques. The strategy might also provide incentives to perform at high levels.

It's very important to offer competitive packages for your labor market, especially when you're vying with your competitors for the best of the labor pool. An effective, well-planned compensation program can increase business results, decrease turnover, increase motivation and help the company achieve its strategic objectives. Again, this means getting the right people for the right price in the right place at the right time.

Example: *Carlos is working with the IT Director, Lionel, on a strategy for hiring independent consultant Anthony as a permanent, full-time employee. Anthony has been making $50 per hour, or $104,00 per year, as a consultant. Lionel assumes he needs to make that same salary to take a permanent job with the company.*

Carlos explains, however, that this isn't necessarily the case. As a consultant, Anthony needed that $50 per hour to supply his own computer equipment and his own retirement plan; he had to supply his own health insurance and insurance for his family members; and his vacation time wasn't paid. In addition, if Anthony accepts the offer for a full-time position, he would be relocating to a geographic region with a lower cost of living. Carlos shows Lionel salary survey data, including comparisons with similar jobs within the company, and explains that a salary of $90,000 would be fair compensation for Anthony's job duties and skills.

WHAT you need to know

Sometimes you can justify paying more than is budgeted for a position if the value that employee brings to the company outweighs the cost. This is an ideal situation to make a business case, as discussed in Chapter 3. HR and the line manager need to consider the skills the employee brings to the company, what the competitive compensation environment is for this person's skills, what it would cost the company to lose this person to a competing company and what resources would be needed to replace that person and get someone else trained and up to speed.

Example: *Carlos is working with Lionel on strategy for hiring the other independent consultant, LaDonna, as a permanent employee. She'd been making $40 per hour as a consultant. They review how LaDonna's contributions to the department would help achieve the company's strategic objectives, and their analysis predicts that LaDonna could indeed complete a vital IT project in two weeks. This project would allow a key new product launch to occur in two months instead of eight months. In addition, the high-level performance potential for LaDonna demonstrates high value and would give the company a competitive advantage in the marketplace.*

Therefore, Carlos recommends that Lionel offer LaDonna $90,000 per year. Lionel looks at his department's budget, however, and sees that he only has $75,000 budgeted for new hires, so he asks why he's allowed to offer more than what's budgeted. Carlos discusses LaDonna's obvious strategic long-term value to the company, and explains that you don't want to lose a high performer of that caliber, especially to the competition. Even though they'd be offering $15,000 more than is budgeted, the potential payback is much higher in terms of revenue brought in through the faster product-to-market time.

In addition, they must consider the cost of recruiting, hiring and training someone else. They must also consider how long it would take to get a different person up to the level of skill that LaDonna already has—if it would take three months, for example, that sets the new product launch behind that much further and consequently delays the revenue flow and competitive advantage. In this instance, a business case for paying $90,000 instead of $75,000 can be made.

Factors for developing your compensation strategy

A compensation plan should be viewed as the *total* compensation package. Employees view the total compensation package as a way to achieve a certain lifestyle, to accumulate wealth, to ensure security and to boost self-esteem.

Employers tend to view the total compensation package as a cost or an investment. However, strategic-thinking employers also view total compensation as a competitive advantage because a well-designed package will allow companies to attract and retain top talent while giving employees the incentive to reach high levels of productivity.

To develop your compensation strategy, ask yourself these questions: How do we design the organization and manage the pay systems needed to attract, retain and motivate the type of talent our company needs? And how is the compensation package going to align with organizational strategy?

DON'T
miss
this

According to Robert J. Greene, Ph.D., author of the Society for Human Resources Management (SHRM) white paper, "Managing Direct Compensation" (©SHRM), strategies must fit the environmental and organizational realities, corporate culture and the organization's structure. Compensation strategies are effective only if they are aligned with the company's strategic business objectives.

Environmental and organizational realities. Greene notes that the political, social and regulatory situations in which the company is involved impact the kind of compensation system that is acceptable to employees. The state of the economy, which includes availability of employees with critical skills, also affects what the company must pay potential workers.

Corporate culture. Compensation structure has an impact on corporate culture. Culture reflects the values of a company to outsiders and to employees. Corporate culture creates expectations and influences how people conduct their business, adapt and learn. Culture can influence styles of thinking, acting and communicating to meet the expectations of the group—ideally, the expectations of the group are the same: to achieve the company's strategic objectives. This influence can, if used properly in the correct context, lead to better performance.

WHAT you need to know

> The way a company rewards its employees is a strong indicator of corporate values and beliefs, according to Brent Longnecker, President of Resources Consulting Group. The correlation between rewards and values can range across compensation strategies. Heavy use of stock options, for example, would imply a belief in company growth. Reimbursement for education would show an emphasis on personal growth. Paid childcare could emphasize the value of family.

Generally, American workers think in terms of individual income and fair rules for everyone. This can cause resistance when, for example, an employer wants to implement work teams paid based on collective results, especially with employees who have many years of service. Your culture may be accustomed to individual achievement for rewards and recognition. Some employees are used to time-based pay, so if you want to implement a business plan to tie pay more closely to performance, this could cause cultural conflict.

Start with an assessment of the present or desired corporate culture. Is the purpose of the compensation strategy to reinforce or shift the corporate culture? Understanding the desired culture and the intent of the compensation strategy allows you to better link the compensation strategy to worker performance.

Remember, corporate culture is a decision factor for individuals seeking employment and in keeping employees once they're employed. For your company to attract and retain top talent, that talent must be comfortable with the people around them and share common beliefs, including the direction of your company.

The organization's structure. The manner in which people are paid affects the staffing and employee development strategies. It's imperative that no conflict exists with the kind of people hired, the positions in which they're placed and the way they're paid.

For example, Green explains, if employees are hired for their interpersonal skills and are trained to place the customer first, but are paid based on how long they have been in the job, the alignment of the HR strategies will be poor and the company likely will not achieve the desired results from those employees.

DON'T miss this

Using salary ranges to establish competitiveness

Using a job grade structure that reflects equity for your job structure, you can use prevailing market levels to establish salary ranges. If your company has decided on a competitive position that sets pay ranges at relevant labor market levels, the market average or medians can help determine your salary ranges. You also can use the relevant market levels if your company position is to pay either above or below prevailing levels, such as when a high-tech corporation might choose to pay above prevailing salaries for research positions that require highly skilled scientists in a competitive market.

Salary ranges have a minimum, midpoint and maximum. The midpoint is the targeted pay level for employees in that grade who perform at acceptable levels. The midpoint is usually set at a level that reflects the average of the market rates, unless the competitive position of the company is to pay above or below market value.

Types of base pay structures

Base salary is typically the cornerstone of any compensation package. This usually is the key piece in the average compensation package. An employer can use several types of base pay structures:

Time-based pay structure. When an employee's pay rate is based only on how long he or she has held a job, the employer can have difficulty controlling payroll costs and motivating employees to perform well. That means salary costs rise for your company without necessarily producing any increase in performance or productivity in working toward the company's strategic objectives. It also sends a signal to employees that performance doesn't matter.

In addition, if longevity is what is rewarded, most employees at some point will reach the top pay rate of their grade, and then often complain that they only receive small or no raises.

An advantage of time-based pay is that it allows a company to predict costs with more certainty than it could using merit pay. It also can avoid difficulties with performance evaluations, depending on how the company has structured its appraisal program.

✓ ✓ *Checklist*

**Time-based pay works best
under the following conditions:**

☐ When many jobs are repetitive and routine, with small variation in performance possible.

☐ When a collective bargaining relationship exists and a high level of trust does not exist between the union leadership and company management.

☐ When employees don't believe managers are able or willing to fairly administer a merit program.

☐ When budgetary limitations or customer rate pressures limit resources and require predictable costs.

☐ When there is concern about potential litigation or employee disagreement regarding performance appraisal ratings and the size of pay increase.

Robert J. Green, "Managing Direct Compensation," April 2003 SHRM White Paper, copyright Society of Human Resources Management, www.shrm.org.

Variable timing step-rate programs. This type of program allows managers to recommend double step increases or early step increases for employees whose performance significantly exceeds standards. It also lets managers deny or delay the step increase when performance doesn't meet expectations.

This system can help companies acknowledge exceptional performance. It requires performance standards so that individual performance is credibly measured with those standards.

On the downside, this system provides a limited number of choices in the size and frequency of increases. Also, if a formal performance appraisal system doesn't exist, the option to vary the size of increases can result in accusations of discrimination.

WHAT you need to know

Combination step-rate/merit pay programs. Some companies have many employees in jobs that have relatively standard learning times, but performance can vary significantly once the job skills are learned. A combined approach provides step increases to the range midpoint based on time. Once the employee reaches the midpoint, further increases may be subject to a performance test.

This combined approach can be advantageous if the employer finds it difficult to differentiate between employees based on performance while they're learning the job. Once an employee is paid at the midpoint, future raises are then based on higher levels of performance. Conversely, employees whose performance declines below the level that justifies their pay rates would receive no raise, a small raise or less frequent raises.

DON'T miss this

Merit pay programs. These performance-based programs use pay ranges with no predefined steps. The range midpoint typically is the targeted level for "meets performance standards." Often, "penetration points" are defined within a range for each performance level and rate at which any worker's pay rate moves to when they reach a performance target. A sound performance appraisal system is key to a successful merit pay program.

Individual-based pay programs. This type of program pays employees for what they *can do* rather than what they *are doing*. The most appropriate applications for this type of system are situations in which the work is highly independent, cooperative behavior is required, work assignment flexibility is needed and the skills or knowledge used is reasonably stable.

> *Example 1: A pharmaceutical company pays a scientific researcher for the relevant knowledge she commands, even though for extended periods of time the work performed doesn't require these qualifications.*
>
> *Example 2: A construction contractor pays a carpenter for the number of job-related skills he has mastered, even though some of them may be rarely used.*

With this system, it's important that skills and knowledge can be defined and that mastery can be determined reliably using unbiased criteria. It's also important to make sure employers get a payback; the average pay levels typically will rise as employees mature in their work. If you have this kind of compensation system, look for some offsetting benefits such as lower staffing levels or increased time-to-market for the company's products.

Types of variable compensation programs

In addition to direct compensation, or pay rates, a total compensation package often includes incentives and rewards. These come into play when recruiting and retaining talented employees who are getting lucrative offers from competitors. Most incentive programs use a percentage of a base pay that will be paid for meeting the business plan and established objectives, and scales are created to allow for incentive awards that are less or more than the target.

Short-term incentive compensation

Short-term incentives are also referred to as bonuses, annual incentives or variable pay. These incentives typically are tied to achieving certain performance targets set for the company or the individual.

The manner in which performance is measured and rewarded has an impact on the types of incentives you may want to offer. If your company wants to get individual behaviors and results, some type of individual incentive program would be most practical. If, however, your work is of a highly independent nature or cooperative behaviors are needed, some form of group incentive would likely be a good approach.

Green identifies two types of individual incentive approaches:
◆ Lump-sum bonuses recognizing performance.
◆ Cash incentive awards to supplement base pay increases for outstanding performance.

Some group incentive approaches include:
◆ **Gainsharing.** These are formula-based programs that use measures such as productivity or cost and which share gains with employees.
◆ **Cash profit sharing.** These are formula-based plans in which employees share a percentage of the profit.
◆ **Group or unit objectives.** These are objective-based plans that identify criteria, set standards and measure results against standards.

Long-term incentive compensation

Long-term incentives do not vest during the next year and, in fact, typically do not vest for three to five years. Usually long-term incentives are awarded as a result of service over time. Because they reward performance over time, long-term incentives are designed to retain talent. For these incentives normal practice is to stagger the vesting time so that early departing employees lose their rights to payouts of equity or cash that may already have been promised.

Long-term incentives often are used for executive compensation programs, although they can be used for any employees. Most programs are cash-based plans or equity-based programs. Cash-based plans are similar to short-term incentive plans except that the measurement period or payout frequency is longer than one year.

Equity-based plans can be complex and generally are comprised of three types:

- ◆ **Purchase plans** enable employees to buy stock, often helped by the company and sometimes at a price below fair market value.
- ◆ **Grant/restricted stock plans** award stock to selected employees without any cash investment required of the employees. These are usually used for senior executives.
- ◆ **Option plans** are popular because the equity markets are, in essence, funding the gain realized by executives, and often these gains never have to be charged against earnings. Options only have value if the price appreciates. Note that many companies are establishing corporate governance policies and giving due attention to ethical matters as a result of the Sarbanes-Oxley Act of 2002 that was enacted following corporate misconduct such as the Enron scandal.

Types of benefits programs

Employers generally offer the same types of benefits as part of their total compensation package, including:

- ◆ **Health insurance**—for illness and injuries.
- ◆ **Disability insurance**—for the employee if an event leaves him or her unable to work.
- ◆ **Death benefits**—for financial security for the employee's family in the event of death.
- ◆ **Retirement benefits**—to help support the employee when he or she retires.
- ◆ **Paid holidays and vacations**—for time off for social and leisure activities.
- ◆ **Educational assistance**—for opportunity to grow personally and professionally.
- ◆ **Sick/Personal Days**—for time away when employees are sick or need to help an ill family member.

Many employers add other benefits as part of their competitive strategy to attract and keep talent. These can include vision insurance, dental insurance, extra paid time off or other benefits that support workers' health and lifestyles.

Types of perquisites

The balance of the kinds of benefits, amenities, perks and rewards that comprise part of the total compensation package are called perquisites. Perquisites typically are less tangible. Employees often place a higher value on perquisites than it costs the company to provide them, according to Longnecker.

Perquisites can range from golf club memberships to subsidized parking. The types of perquisites offered to executives and the rest of the employee population differ.

Examples of perquisites can include:

- ◆ Adoption assistance programs.
- ◆ Bus/transportation reimbursement.
- ◆ Casual dress code.
- ◆ Cell phone.
- ◆ Childcare services.
- ◆ Company car.
- ◆ Company picnics and parties.
- ◆ Concierge service.
- ◆ Direct deposit.
- ◆ Dry cleaning service.
- ◆ Employee Appreciation Day.
- ◆ Employee of the Year award.
- ◆ Financial planning assistance.
- ◆ Flexible scheduling.
- ◆ Free coffee, soda and water.
- ◆ Free massages.
- ◆ Free snacks.
- ◆ Golf club membership.
- ◆ Health club membership.
- ◆ Job sharing.
- ◆ Laptop computers.
- ◆ Loan programs and salary advances.
- ◆ Online benefits management.
- ◆ Paid time off to perform community service.
- ◆ Pleasant corporate culture.
- ◆ Scholarship referral services.
- ◆ Seats at sporting events.
- ◆ Support groups.

- ◆ Subsidized parking.
- ◆ Training and development opportunities.
- ◆ Wellness program.
- ◆ Work anniversary gifts.

A⁺ *Best Practices*

Lenscrafters' perquisites align with the HR strategy

Lenscafters/Luxottica Retail's mission is to "Create exceptional value in the lives of our customers, associates and shareholders. We will do this by enthusiastically satisfying every customer all the time and creating an environment where our associates can fulfill their personal dreams." The HR strategy is to create a workplace that attracts, develops and retains world-class associates (the company does not use the word employees), and their official mission is "To become the world's best workplace." To that end, the company offers perquisite benefits that include:

- ◆ 24-hour health information from Nurseline service.
- ◆ Anniversary award program.
- ◆ Best of the Best award (coveted award associates work for all year—they call it their own version of the Academy Awards®).
- ◆ Childcare discount.
- ◆ Credit union membership.
- ◆ Discounts on eye exams and glasses.
- ◆ Employee Assistance Program (EAP).
- ◆ Friends & Family coupons for 50 percent off eyewear.
- ◆ Gift of Sight Program (allows associates to provide eye exams & glasses to the needy).
- ◆ Give A Day Program (donating time off to another associate).
- ◆ Guardian Angel Fund.
- ◆ Horizon Club (associates who have received top recognition get $1,000 and are flown to headquarters in Cincinnati to be honored at a special awards dinner).

- Lab Olympics (honors stores with the best results in labs—everyone at headquarters goes outside to greet the bus bringing the winners).
- Laser eye correction discount.
- Platinum Service Award.
- President's Pin Program (pins awarded when customers send letters).
- Shining Star awards.
- Spirit of Diversity Award.
- Wow-grams (thank-yous from other associates).

Communicating your strategies

The most important way to tie the compensation plan to the company's strategic plan is through effective communication. Longnecker stresses that without communication, the compensation plan won't be a part of corporate culture. Strong communication keeps managers and employees focused on the same goals and helps workers understand how their compensation relates to their professional development and their roles in achieving the company's strategic objectives.

Communication also helps build trust in HR so that employees and managers are more willing to engage HR in discussions in the future and feel more confident about HR's decisions.

Communication is the only way to make the strategy effective and successful. Employees will feel more comfortable with their total compensation package if they understand the overall strategy. When compensation plans are not communicated clearly, employees may feel they're underpaid or are not receiving the same benefits as others.

DON'T
miss
this

Not only do employees need to know the specifics of the compensation strategy, they need to hear it more than once. This is especially true for incentive plans—it's imperative that employees understand what's expected of them. Take time to follow up with employees to ensure that they fully understand the programs, and don't wait to do it only at performance appraisal time.

Gaining line manager support and understanding

Obviously, a key to your compensation communication program is your line manager. Your managers have to understand the company's strategic objectives, as well as to understand and support your compensation strategies and how they fit into the company's strategy. And they have to understand and support you when changes are made to compensation structures that need to be communicated to their employees.

One challenge HR professionals constantly face is getting line managers to understand the total compensation strategy. Some managers' eyes start glazing over when discussion starts about midpoints and market rates and other statistical factors. Some supervisors tend to manage as a "friend" and lean toward fighting for the employees' wants no matter what the company's strategy might be. Other managers just don't think it's part of their job to be involved with compensation strategy.

WHAT you need to know

Explain to your line managers how the total compensation plan is structured and why, how much the company spends on the total compensation package, and how compensation affects the company's bottom line.

Managers might not realize that base pay rates are a fixed cost, so that when they give someone an increase to a base pay rate, that fixed cost increases on a permanent basis. Talk about dollars and tie the information to the business results and how the increase affects the entire organization.

Example: An employer's total employee compensation costs are $10 million annually. The majority of managers want to give their employees raises that would increase the total compensation costs by 3 percent, or $300,000, annually. The managers—and the employees—believe an annual 3 percent increase is akin to a cost-of-living increase, almost an entitlement.

If the employer's operating income margin is 10 percent, then the company has to earn an additional $3 million in annual revenue to cover the $300,000 increase in compensation fixed costs. This increase in fixed compensation costs, then, affects the new revenue hurdles that must be overcome by the product development, marketing, sales, production and customer service functions in the organization.

It's HR's role to clearly explain to supervisors why compensation plans are structured as they are, and it's the supervisors' role to support the company and have those conversations with the employees. In that conversation, the supervisor must help the employee see the bigger picture.

It's your role to give managers and supervisors the tools they need to communicate effectively on compensation and reward issues so that the entire workforce—HR, management and employees—understands how all the organization's activities, including the compensation structures, are designed to support the business objectives.

You might also find yourself in situations in which the line manager comes to you with a new position and has already decided what the pay rate should be. This is an opportunity for you to be strategic with respect to compensation and to educate the line manager on how he or she can think strategically as well:

- ◆ Find out why the supervisor thinks the salary should be at the level he or she is suggesting. Knowing the motivation and concerns behind the supervisor's salary recommendation will be useful in helping the supervisor understand the big picture. You'll learn more about how the company actually functions from supervisors than you will from the "senior strategists" and, as HR, it's your job to bring the two into alignment.

◆ Share the salary survey data you've gathered for that position, comparable job descriptions, information about comparable internal jobs and any other information you use to determine the pay rate. This will demonstrate that you're not pulling numbers out of the air.

◆ Show the manager how setting a certain base salary also includes benefits, how many dollars that translates to and how it affects the manager's department budget, as well as the company's profits. While you can expect that the supervisor will understand the impact on his or her own budget, it's less likely that the supervisor will understand the long-term organizational impact of a salary adjustment and how this impacts the company's business plan. Be prepared to use examples.

◆ Explain how you're applying this compensation strategy across the entire company, not just in his or her department or for only that one position.

◆ Reiterate the company's overall strategic objectives. This information will help the manager see the bigger picture.

Example: *Isaac meets with HR and asks for a $10,000 raise for his engineer Michael, who says he's going to quit if he doesn't get the $10,000 because he can make $10,000 more at another company.*

Non-strategic approach: *HR tells Isaac that the $10,000 is not in the budget and there's nothing they can do.*

Strategic approach: *HR talks with Isaac to find out more about Michael's situation. Is it only the money making him consider leaving, or is he unhappy about some other aspect of his job or the company? What kind of performer is Michael? Stellar? Average? How much influence does he have over others in the workplace? Why did Michael even start looking at other opportunities? Employees rarely leave only because of compensation. Are there problems in Isaac's department? Is it understaffed? Has Michael reached a dead-end in his career?*

HR then examines the business case for this situation with Isaac. Would Michael's new job offer tuition reimbursement? If not, that's $4,000 worth of value beyond his base salary that the company provides that his new employer wouldn't. Does the new employer offer subsidized parking? If not, that's another $1,000 per year the company provides that the new company wouldn't. Does the other company offer subsidized childcare? Then that's another $3,000 of value the company offers that the new company doesn't. Assuming that these benefits have value to Michael—and that he either utilizes them now or will in the future—that's $7,000 in value that the company may not be paying in direct salary, but that Michael receives now and wouldn't at the new company—effectively cutting his gain from the other company to $3,000.

And what about flexible schedules, casual dress, incentive bonuses, dental insurance and other benefits the company now offers? If not matched by the prospective employer, these likely would cut Michael's potential gain even further. So what is Michael really looking for? Recognition? Power? Opportunity for advancement? More training? More travel? More time off? What can HR do to help Michael remain a motivated, productive employee?

HR is fulfilling its strategic role when it addresses all the potential issues in a compensation-related (or other tactical area) question to make sure that all employees are contributing to the company's success.

WHAT you need to know

Answering the question, "Why is this my pay rate?"

No HR professional gets through a career without having to answer questions from employees about why they're being paid a certain rate instead of something higher. Whether it's you or the line manager who has that conversation with the employee, the answer should not be, "Because that's the budget." That is not the strategic approach.

The strategic approach is to discuss the total compensation package—the value of the base pay, variable pay (incentives), benefits and perquisites:

◆ Share the data that was used to develop the pay structure for that employee's job.

◆ Demonstrate how that employee's compensation package is competitive in your industry in your geographical region for that type of job.

◆ Show how that employee's compensation fits in with compensation structure of the company.

◆ Illustrate how the compensation structure is designed to motivate the employee for professional development, for high achievement and for helping the company meet its strategic objectives.

WHAT you need to know

It also can be a good practice to review the job duties compared to the job description and make sure the employee is in the appropriate grade level. Sometimes you actually may find that the person's job has moved beyond what the job description says, and that the description and pay level need adjustment.

A⁺ Best Practices

Answering the question, "Why is this my pay rate?"

Yolanda seems upset as she approaches the HR manager. Yolanda says that she's been researching her job on the Internet and found a web site that says she should be making $125,000, but she's only making $100,000. She doesn't think that's right. Yolanda is obviously agitated, but it's unclear whether she's angry, disillusioned, vengeful or a combination of those emotions.

HR's strategic response begins with a quiet, fact-based discussion about the quality of the data that Yolanda found on the Internet. Where did it come from? Is it a web site that helps people find jobs and negotiate salaries? Is that $125,000 figure an average of salaries input by other visitors to the site, or did the site itself conduct surveys? Is the salary based on a job description (actual duties performed) or a title (which can have varied meaning between companies)? What geographical region was represented by that $125,000 figure, or were geographic regions even designated?

The HR manager also reiterates the company's strategic objectives, explaining how the overall compensation strategy fits into the big picture. HR explains what salary data it uses to set the range for Yolanda's specific job. HR's strategic discussion is an attempt to educate and provide context to Yolanda's understandable confusion about how much her job is worth. Consequently, HR also talks about the cost of living versus the cost of labor.

Additionally, HR might also offer to review Yolanda's job description, which is used when setting compensation levels, to make sure it matches the duties she actually is performing. HR will also explain the dollar values of the benefits and perquisites Yolanda receives.

WHAT you need to know

Sometimes, particularly if relocation is involved, you may want to explain about the cost of living and the cost of labor for the region in which the employee will work. The cost of living is how much an employee would need to earn to maintain a certain style of living. Cost of labor is how much the company would have to pay for a particular position in a particular job market. Sometimes those numbers differ.

For example, the cost of living in an urban area may be a higher percentage than the cost of labor. If your company uses the cost of labor as a factor in determining your compensation structure, employees may argue that they deserve the cost of living percentage instead. That is another opportunity to have a strategic discussion and explain the company's philosophy for using the cost of labor versus the cost of living.

Understanding your company's strategic objectives, building those into your compensation structure and clearly communicating those plans to your line managers and employees are keys to a successful strategic compensation plan.

The Quiz

1. Which of the following is not a goal of strategic compensation plans?
   a. Attracting, retaining and motivating employees.
   b. Investing in desired behaviors and getting desired results.
   c. Spending as much money as possible for labor costs.
   d. Helping employees understand and work toward the company's strategic objectives.
   e. Maintaining a competitive edge in the competition for talent in a limited labor pool.

2. Short-term incentive compensation programs are designed for individuals to achieve performance targets set in alignment with the company's strategic objectives. ❏ True   ❏ False

3. Long-term incentive compensation programs function to retain talent over a long period of time. ❏ True   ❏ False

4. What is a perquisite?
   a. A required course needed to get a college degree.
   b. A mosquito-like insect typically found in the Northwest U.S.
   c. Benefits, perks and rewards beyond traditional insurance, retirement and time-off benefits.

5. Effective communication about compensation programs helps keep managers and employees focused on the same goals and helps employees understand how their compensation relates to their professional development and their roles in achieving the company's strategic objectives. ❏ True   ❏ False

Answer key: 1. c; 2. T; 3. T; 4. c; 5. T

Strategic benefits

Kira is the recruiter for a major wholesale lumber company. Her organization has determined that it needs a more experienced sales force. To meet that goal, Kira has been asked to hire three new salespeople who already have a minimum of 20 years in sales work.

The salary the company is offering is more than competitive but Kira wants to make sure that the benefits package she presents is inviting to these experienced workers who the company wants to hire.

After interviewing 12 applicants and asking about desirable benefits, Kira realizes that a prescription plan and flexible work hours are the two most appealing benefits to the people in the age group she wants to bring into the company.

The next step is to find out how feasible it will be to provide those two benefits.

Aren't benefits part of compensation?

WHAT you need to know

Most employee benefits specialists can tell you that strategic benefits management has changed over the past few years. Randall Abbott, Regional Practice Leader and Senior Consultant in Watson Wyatt's Group Benefits and Health Care Consulting Practice, discusses some of the challenges employers face in designing and implementing benefits packages in today's ever-changing workplace.

Three major challenges exist today. First, contextually, benefits used to be seen as an appendage to compensation strategy—a necessary evil to attract and retain employees. Today, benefits are being viewed as a strategic component of total pay. Simply put, the value of direct pay plus the value of the employer's funding toward the benefits package are seen as linked.

From management's perspective, benefits are also taking on a new role as a vehicle for improving workforce health and productivity. A healthier, productive workforce means more unimpaired workdays, which means more productivity with no increase in direct or indirect labor costs. The math is simple: we can reduce our unit cost of labor by upping productivity or reducing labor costs. Properly crafted, today's health care, disability and lost time programs can positively impact productivity and reduce costs.

Second, vendor services and vendor management are recurring complaints among managers nationwide. Service is terrible, costs are high and employee or patient complaints seem to arise hourly. It's less of an issue with plans that are less utilized, such as life and disability plans, but it's a huge issue in medical, dental, drug, EAP, mental health and any type of outsourced plan.

Plus, costs are going up. Employers feel like they're paying more for less and see no end in sight. The biggest problem with many vendors is accountability. It's the "other guy" syndrome. Nobody wants to take responsibility. That's why we push hard for common sense performance goals and clear, simple accountabilities for results. It's not magic: it's good vendor management.

Third, benefit delivery has changed. It's not just about clerks processing claims or insurers assuming risk. The old paradigms don't always work today—old measures don't always make sense. For example, the past five years have seen a shift from more self-funding to more insurance. HMOs are being embraced where we fought 10 years ago to keep them out.

Similarly, the metrics (or the ways we measure success) have changed. It used to be that paying 80 percent of claims in 10 days was great. Now, with 25 to 50 percent of claims transmitted electronically and 25 to 35 percent of claims being autoadjudicated with no human involvement, that metric doesn't make sense.

In addition, delivery isn't just selecting an insurer to pay claims anymore. The benefits manager must consider design parameters, a host of risk transfer techniques, various funding arrangements, carve-outs, managed care networks and care delivery protocols, plus a myriad of disability management techniques, to name a few. Now electronic commerce and the new HIPAA electronic data transfer rules effective in February 2000 add a further complication.

Traditionally, benefits were viewed as just another part of the compensation package offered to employees. Currently, the trend is to look at benefits as a separate entity—one that is used by organizations to hire and retain the best employees and one that is watched over carefully to get the most benefits for the dollars spent. And because benefits are such an important hiring and retention tool, employers are making an effort to provide benefit choices so that the benefits received by employees are tailored for their needs. This diversity may be provided by offering a menu of benefits from which employees may select or by offering different levels of coverage, depending on need.

Worst case scenario

Rosa works for the Knott Company. The Knott Company prides itself on its benefits package and is surprised when Rosa announces her intention to leave because the benefits are better at another company.

What's wrong at the Knott Company? They provided Rosa with full family health care coverage, sick child day care reimbursement, tuition reimbursement and a plan that provides legal services. Wouldn't anyone welcome those benefits? Not someone who can't use them! Look at the benefits package from Rosa's point of view:

◆ Rosa is single. The deductible on her full-family health care is more than she spends for an annual physical and she is blessed with good health. All of her health care cost, therefore, is out of pocket.

◆ Since Rosa currently has no children, child care reimbursement is also of no use to her.

◆ Rosa has a Ph.D. and does not plan on further education, so tuition reimbursement is not a benefit for her.

◆ And, being a lawyer herself, Rosa does not have a need for employer-paid legal services.

Solution: If the Knott Company offered a choice of health care options and other benefits, Rosa could select benefits that are meaningful to her—something that might prompt her to stay on at the Knott Company where she is otherwise a satisfied employee. For example:

◆ Less expensive individual health care coverage with a lower deductible and premiums.

◆ A choice between the child care benefit and membership in a wellness/fitness center.

◆ Money toward education or towards computer purchases.

◆ Prepaid legal services or prepaid financial planning services.

Whichever specific benefits an organization decides to offer, they should be varied enough to be meaningful to a diverse workforce. Keep in mind that the best benefit for one employee may be useless to another. Look for groups of benefits that employees can choose from that are similar in cost or expense, but diverse in what they provide.

Where should you begin in deciding what benefits to offer? Take some time to assess your organization's current benefit usage. Don't get lured by hot benefits or benefit fads. Think long-term and build in the opportunity to change benefits should a benefit or two become obsolete. Think about how much a benefit might cost in the future—will it still be something you can offer? Taking time to think through and build a strategic benefit plan will serve you well for the long term.

✓ Checklist

Designing a strategic benefits package

Here are some issues to consider in helping your organization design a strategic benefits package—that is, one that meets the needs of your workforce, serves your hiring and retention goals and makes sense for your bottom line:

☐ Take a demographic snapshot of your workforce to help understand the needs of your employees. Be sure to capture different employee constituencies, if applicable, to determine if you should be aware of any specific patterns. For example, "Baby Boomers" may have the need for retirement planning benefits and more medical care needs than when they were younger. Or perhaps you have a young workforce that needs child-care benefits. Or employees in the "sandwich" generation that need elder care benefits.

☐ Review your organization's policies, benefits and programs to determine what is currently offered.

☐ Measure usage of existing benefit programs.

☐ Compare the fit between existing programs and your workforce's current and projected needs. If differing employee needs surfaced in the demographic snapshot, make sure your comparative analysis also considers these groups.

Continued on next page

Continued from previous page

☐ Identify new policies and programs or fine-tune existing policies and programs.
☐ Consider organization culture and workflows to ensure proposed new policies and programs will be supported in the work environment.
☐ Stress the availability of useful benefits and programs.
☐ Make sure you put your benefit dollars where they will bring you the most value.

Offer benefits in variety packs

The growth of benefits and services in the workplace has corresponded with the changing and growing needs of employees, while at the same time benefit budgets are tight. That is the biggest challenge for benefits managers. It is also the greatest opportunity to meet the needs of employees. In the changing workforce the needs of every employee may be different, and a well planned benefits and services program can offer solutions to many of the problems or needs each individual employee may face.

To meet your strategy of hiring and retaining the best employees while holding down costs, consider a variety of benefits. Remember that to be effective benefits do not have to be expensive, they have to be meaningful to the employee—something that the employee can really use to improve his or her life.

Worst case scenario

The employee benefits satisfaction survey that your company has done the last several years has revealed an increasing dissatisfaction with the benefits your company offers. Your company has for years offered a traditional pension plan, a traditional health plan and a good vacation package.

Solution: If your benefits plan was designed to meet the needs of the traditional stereotypical employee of many years ago—male, married with wife and children—then it may not have kept pace with the changing dynamics of your workforce. Today, your employee demographics probably encompass that traditional stereotypical employee, along with married females who are part of a two-income couple with or without children, married males who are part of a two-income couple with or without children and single employees who may or may not have children.

To meet the demands of such a diverse employee population, you may want to consider a "cafeteria" approach to providing benefits. Employees are given a specific value for the amount of benefits that they may choose from a menu of different items. This means that employees may have the option to take the cash as compensation, in lieu of selecting any benefits, or may select a customized benefits package from pensions, group insurance, childcare, time-off or other offerings.

With a flexible benefit plan, the employee can pick the benefits he or she wants, provided the employee's allotted maximum dollar value is not exceeded.

A good benefits program is a flexible program. The more flexible the program is, the more your employees can tailor their choices to meet their genuine needs. One popular approach to meeting the changing benefit needs of employees is the flexible or cafeteria plan arrangement. This type of plan allows the employee to modify his or her choices to meet different needs (for example, life insurance, legal services, medical insurance, etc.) and adjust to meet those needs over a period of time (such as changes in age or marital and family status).

Remember Kira's plan to use benefits that will appeal to older workers from the opening scenario? A flexible benefit plan allows you to offer a variety of benefits so that you can provide meaningful choices for a wide range of needs and interests.

WHAT you need to know

What is a cafeteria plan/flex plan?

A cafeteria plan/flex plan offers employees a choice between cash and benefits or among several benefits. These plans are permitted under Section 125 of the Internal Revenue Code.

The choices can be:
1. Among different levels of the same benefit (such as different health plans); or
2. Among different types of benefits (such as between life insurance, dental insurance and cash).

In order for a plan to be a cafeteria plan and keep its tax-favored status under Code Sec. 125, the plan must:

◆ Permit employees to choose between two or more benefits, consisting of at least one nontaxable benefit and cash;
◆ Be a written plan;
◆ Be for employees only (that is, allow only employees to participate);
◆ Not include any benefit that defers the receipt of compensation; and
◆ Require participants to make annual benefit elections.

These choices may be structured as individual plans, as modular combinations of plans or as a core of basic benefits plus options.

Advantages to employees. Offering a flexible "cafeteria" benefit program to your employees has these advantages:

◆ Employees are offered the chance to select their benefits based on their needs;
◆ Benefits may be offered on a pretax basis;
◆ The longer-service employee may be interested in pensions;

- One-half of a two-worker family may not be interested in any group insurance at all; and
- The single employee without dependents may want extra vacation time.

Advantages to employers. Besides being able to meet the needs of different individual employees, the flexible approach also has benefits for the employer. For employers, the advantages include:

- Employers can manage or limit benefit costs by setting their contributions at a specific level.
- A flexible plan can serve to break the long-term trend of stacking more and more benefits on top of each other—a trend that only adds more expense.
- Flex allows employers to "move" employees toward more efficient plans without the negative reaction that could occur when benefits are reduced or eliminated.
- Flexible plans create the illusion, through having more choices, that the employer is providing more benefits without necessarily increasing costs.
- Companies with flexible benefit packages report less turnover and have a recruiting advantage.
- Because the program is less paternalistic than a traditional program where the employer makes all the decisions for every employee, flexible plans can also have a positive impact on a company's image. Trusting employees to know their own needs and allowing them to choose their compensation package can make a conservative company seem innovative.
- Flex can link employee compensation and corporate performance with benefit choices.
- Consolidating benefit programs in merger or acquisition situations may be easier when flex plans are used.

The flexible benefit approach is an extension of the theory that employees will respond better when they are treated as individuals and when they have a say in making decisions about their work lives.

DON'T
miss
this

WHAT
you need
to know

A cafeteria plan may offer the following taxable benefits, but only on an *after-tax* basis (because these have no related specific tax exclusion):

◆ Long-term disability insurance (but only if proceeds are not taxable to the beneficiary when received);

◆ Group-term life insurance coverage in excess of $50,000 face amount;

◆ Dependent life insurance;

◆ Contributions to a nondiscriminatory profit-sharing or stock bonus plan;

◆ Benefits under group legal services;

◆ Long-term care coverage for employees, their parents or their in-laws; or

◆ Car insurance, homeowners' insurance or other personal insurance programs on a group basis.

Some types of benefits are off limits and cannot be offered as part of a cafeteria plan:

◆ Deferred compensation plans that allow employees to carry over unused contributions or benefits;

◆ Educational assistance, scholarships or fellowships;

◆ Tax-exempt fringe benefits such as no-additional-cost services, *de minimis* fringe benefits, working condition fringe benefits or qualified employee benefits;

◆ Reimbursement for medical expenses that are either not deductible (such as cosmetic surgery) or not substantiated;

◆ Health care coverage provided by an entity other than the employer;

◆ Group-term life insurance for spouses or dependents;

◆ Vanpooling;

◆ Company cafeteria benefits or meals and lodging; and

◆ Retirement health benefits for working employees.

Communicating the flexible benefit plan

Information needs for communicating the plan revolve around the complexity of the choices. But keep these guidelines in mind:

- ◆ Communications must be clearer and more concise than with the traditional benefit program so that all choices are understood by employees.
- ◆ Specialists may be needed for answering employee questions, but the increased involvement of employees in choosing their benefits will lead to a greater understanding of the various benefits available.
- ◆ To help employees make the complex calculations involved in the cost/benefit choices, making a computer available is very useful.
- ◆ Emphasize the positive aspects of flexible planning for employees; otherwise, some of your employees may become alienated by the prospect of having to drop some benefits in order to fit into the flexible plan.

Administrative costs

A flexible benefit approach may present some added costs. You may have to do extra bookkeeping. Some related additional administrative costs could come in the form of:

- ◆ Added paperwork;
- ◆ Additional personnel for counseling employees on their benefit choices;
- ◆ Additional time to determine equivalent values under different plans; and
- ◆ Added attention to delivery of information about the flexible system.

Managing employee benefits

The rapid growth of benefits and services in the workplace and the changing needs of employees have greatly increased the need for effective benefits management. It's important to plan and manage a benefits program so that it offers solutions to the needs of individual employees while, at the same time, minimizing the cost of the benefits to your company.

Key concepts in benefits management

Objectives: Benefits need to support the overall strategy and objectives of the company, as well as human resource planning

Leadership: Your company must decide whether the benefits plan will match or lead the competition.

Administration: The role of a benefits manager has expanded in recent years, and more attention than ever is placed on containing costs. Increasingly, benefits administration is being outsourced, allowing for a greater focus on strategy. Cost containment remains a factor in all plans.

Meeting needs of employees

The growth of benefits and services in the workplace has corresponded with the changing and growing needs of employees. This is one of your biggest challenges. It's also a good opportunity to meet the needs of your company's employees.

As your workforce changes, each employee's needs may be different, and a well-planned benefits and services program can offer solutions to many of the problems or needs that an individual employee may face. To achieve the best results in employee motivation and satisfaction, benefits, of course, should be tailored to the genuine needs of employees.

Flexibility is the key to success of any employee benefits program.

In the past, group benefits and pensions were generally designed to meet the needs of a stereotypical employee—male, married with wife and children. Today this type of employee makes up less than one-fifth of the work force. Child care issues, the needs of aging parents and juggling the demands of a two-income family are just some of the complex personal issues that can affect job performance in the absence of an effective benefits plan.

Cost containment

Because of the increasing cost of benefits—both the cost to the employer and to the employee—cost containment has become a key management function. Trimming costs may require redesigning or restructuring health care and other benefit plans or making the employee responsible for more of the cost of the benefits.

Consumer-directed health plans (CDHPs), also called health reimbursement arrangements (HRAs), are one way for employers to combat the impact of rising health care costs. What are health reimbursement arrangements (HRAs)? An HRA is an arrangement that:

1. Is funded solely by the employer and not provided pursuant to salary reduction election or otherwise under a cafeteria plan.
2. Reimburses employees and former employees (including retirees) and their spouses and dependents for medical expenses.
3. Provides reimbursements up to a maximum dollar amount for a coverage period.

Further, any unused portion of the maximum dollar amount at the end of a coverage period is carried forward to increase the maximum reimbursement amount in subsequent coverage periods.

Other cost-cutting measures include coordination of benefits in dual-career families, deductibles and coinsurance. Also, having a third-party administrator handle medical claims can provide health care cost savings.

Communicating with employees about benefits

An employer needs to have effective communication with respect to its benefit plans for several reasons. These include:

- ◆ Attraction and retention of employees;
- ◆ Compliance with laws and regulations; and
- ◆ The bottom line.

Companies spend between 20 and 50 percent of their payroll costs on employee benefits, and they want to make sure that their plans are well understood and utilized effectively—for example, are employees using flexible spending accounts to take advantage of tax savings for health or dependent care costs?

No matter how cost effective a benefit program may be, the program will be useless if employees are unaware of the opportunities it presents to them.

A good communication program will inform employees how much the company is doing for them, allow employees to understand and make use of available benefits and present an opportunity for the company to sell itself to the employees.

The communication process is also very important if any reorganization of the benefit plan is undertaken. Often, the modification of an existing program involves the trading of prior benefits for new coverage. Effective communication becomes a major factor as to whether these benefit tradeoffs are perceived by employees as a positive attempt by the employer to enhance the compensation package, or where appropriate, as a necessary, but painful business decision to reduce costs.

Many communication opportunities—some more formal than others—exist to present a full picture of benefits and service programs to employees. Be sure you are taking advantage of these opportunities.

Here are several triggers for benefits communications—times when you'll want to carefully communicate with employees about their benefits:

- ◆ **Recruitment.** Benefits can be used to attract the more knowledgeable prospective employees during recruitment.
- ◆ **Annual benefit statements.** Annual benefit statements sent to an employee's home are documents that give a personalized rundown of that employee's eligibility for benefits. To maximize its effectiveness, include a letter from management explaining the goals of the employee benefit program, how specific aspects of the program are designed to achieve these goals and where the employee is in relation to these goals.
- ◆ **Discussion with supervisors.** Frequently, employees are more comfortable talking to their supervisors or managers than with upper management or the HR department. That means that discussions with supervisors may present a strategic communication opportunity.

But, exercise caution! Many benefit plans are complex, so you need to educate your managers on when it's appropriate to answer benefits questions, and when it's appropriate to refer the matter to HR.

DON'T miss this

◆ **Publications.** Company publications, such as benefits books or company magazines, provide a ready source for employees who want to keep up-to-date on their benefit plans.

Developing a communications program

The process of creating and delivering solid, well thought-out and effective employee benefits communications is governed by 10 rules.

✓ Checklist

Developing a benefits communication program

1. Know what benefits your organization provides and how they work.
2. Know what your employees think about your benefits program.
3. Understand your organization's business.
4. Understand your organization's culture and values.
5. Understand your employees' values and worth ethics.
6. Get a firm handle on benefits communications and responsibilities.
7. Prepare a benefits communication plan of action.
8. Sell your communication plan to your managers.
9. Select, prepare and distribute benefits communications to fit corporate objectives and employee needs.
10. Evaluate the effectiveness of your benefit communications and apply what you have learned to future communication plans.

In communicating with employees about your benefits program, make a clear connection between the company's goals and objectives and the benefits programs it's offering. Show how benefits affect your financial outlook and how working together with employees to hold down costs while providing a solid benefits package is essential to that financial goal.

Best Practices

Developing a benefits communications program

As is true of many things, perception can be reality when it comes to employee benefit plans. Communication of the employee benefit plan to employees can be critical to the plan's success. The consulting firm of Grant Thornton offers the following tips for developing your communications program:

◆ Use written communication. It will be more effective if accompanied by color leaflets or brochures.

◆ Use an intranet or secure Internet site when you want to provide speedy access for employees. But remember that you may have employees without access to a computer.

◆ Use a presentation for announcing changes to existing plans. Provide a chance to ask questions. Provide handouts.

◆ Make arrangements to communicate with employees unable to attend the presentation.

WHAT you need to know

Use technology to help in the communication of benefits. There are advantages to using the Internet for benefits communication, such as potentially improved accuracy and timeliness, with the information available to employees when they need and want it. Effective online benefits communications should:

◆ Be succinct;
◆ Use short paragraphs and meaningful headings;
◆ Be written in a conversational, informal style;
◆ Use links; and
◆ Minimize the need for scrolling.

Be sure to strike a balance with print. Putting benefits information online does not completely eliminate the need for print communications. Use collateral materials to promote online communication. For example, postcards and reminders are still valuable. And be sure to use print material to reach those employees without computer access.

Getting information up online isn't merely a simple matter of putting print material "as is" in electronic format. Simply dumping print materials online may not be better than doing nothing, because the material likely will not translate well. Keep in mind that people generally don't read online information in a linear fashion. And remember, you need to keep material up-to-date.

Cultivate a communication culture. Syndine Imholte, president of Capstone Communications, Inc., in Los Angeles, speaking at a teleweb seminar sponsored by the International Foundation of Employee Benefit Plans, offered this advice:

Open and honest communication needs to be a way of life in your organization. If that's not where you are right now, don't expect the culture to change overnight. You need to have a communication strategy in place that takes into account your objective, audience, culture, hot buttons, messages, delivery system and media.

Be prepared. Imholte says failure to prepare often leads people to get tongue-tied or to blurt out an unpleasant message.

Consider the following example.

Example: *Chantal, an HR generalist, knows that employees will come to her office after the company spokesperson sets forth the upcoming changes to the health plan. She's concerned about being effective in her communications with these employees. On the one hand, she's an employee too, and she is unhappy about the changes to the health plan. On the other hand, as an HR professional, she understands the business drivers behind the decision to change the plan.*

So, following Imholte's advice, Chantal is ready when Juan comes into her office. Chantal knows that Juan is influential with his fellow employees, so she wants to take advantage of this opportunity. First, she listens as Juan explains how he feels squeezed by having to pay more for less and how he feels like his pay has been cut.

Then Chantal positions her message: "As you have heard on the news, health care costs are way up." She sympathizes

> *with his feeling squeezed, and then she delivers the bottom line gently: "Our health care costs are going up faster than our revenues. In addition, we continue to be very competitive in our industry when it comes to salaries. But if we don't get health costs under control, we're looking at damage to our business and to the careers of our coworkers."*

How much will it cost? Effective communication will require your organization to expend resources—both in terms of dollars and time. But, when budgets are tight, you do have some control over your costs if you don't assume you have to keep doing things the way you've done them in the past. Consider the best practice below, which was reported in the *Houston Chronicle*.

Best Practices

Lower your benefit communication costs

The City of Houston lowered its costs for publications from about $110,000 in 2002 to $43,000 in 2003. How did they accomplish savings of over 50 percent? By taking simple steps—they stopped printing their benefits publications for employees and retirees in color, instead opting for black and white. They changed one publication to online only. Finally, they changed the printing frequency of the benefits publications from bimonthly to quarterly, and they reduced the number of copies printed.

◆ Be organized.

◆ Avoid words or concepts that employees don't understand.

◆ Be sure to explain acronyms.

Making the most of benefit dollars in hard economic times

The cost of providing benefits to employees increases dramatically every year. The cost of all employee benefit payments as a percentage of payroll averages between 20 and 50 percent. As a result, it's essential that benefit dollars be put to their best use.

Benefits are most cost-effective if you provide benefits that are most valued by employees. Benefit systems have tended to grow and change for non-strategic reasons—that is, in response to outside events rather than for the purposes of meeting internal changing employee needs or improving organizational effectiveness. The most frequent example is when similar organizations attempt to duplicate each other's benefit packages. Just because a benefit is good for one company doesn't mean it will be good for your company.

Many companies assume that benefits are more highly valued by employees when they are of high cost to the employer. Remember, most employees don't know what a particular benefit or service costs. By involving employees in what is offered, your benefit package is more likely to be cost-effective in terms of offering the most desired coverage within a given budget. You may even find out that employees prefer some low-cost benefits, such as flex-time, to higher ticket items.

Cost consideration in plan design

Costs can't be contained without first designing benefits to meet individual needs and to permit greater employee involvement in the selection process. Employees who are older and no longer have the costs and responsibilities of a growing family don't need the same services as younger employees who are raising a family.

Consider three basic costs when structuring an employee benefit plan:

◆ Cost to the employer;
◆ Cost to the employee in terms of payroll deductions required to participate in the benefit program; and
◆ Cost to the employee for other out-of-pocket costs the employee incurs to purchase coverage not provided in the benefit (such as health insurance deductibles and coinsurance).

Although not strictly measurable in terms of dollars and cents, the most important cost consideration to employees is the perceived value of a benefit. Any benefit program is a waste of money if the employees perceive no usefulness from the benefits offered. Employee surveys are the best way to gather data on what benefits and services are best suited to individual employees. Employees know what coverage, protections and services they want. In that way the benefit dollar is stretched to full value for both the company and employees. As mentioned previously, make a clear connection between the company's goals and its desire to provide meaningful benefits for its employees. Don't assume everyone will understand that is the message, spell it out and repeat it.

Avoiding overlapping coverage

When evaluating a benefit program, consider mandatory benefits such as Social Security, unemployment compensation and workers' compensation. You will want to avoid providing an unnecessary overlap in these areas of coverage.

Some common benefit programs that can be tailored to avoid overlap include pension plans that are integrated with Social Security and health insurance plans that carve out those eligible for Medicare.

A benefit program that you might not consider as being subject to overlap problems is educational assistance. You can design educational assistance to make it conditional upon the use of available veterans' assistance. It's important to review all programs, not just the "common" ones, for potential overlapping coverage.

Effective cost/program balance

It's no longer prudent to assume that there is little difference in how to distribute compensation expenses between wages and benefits, as long as the total cost remains competitive.

The challenge of future benefit planning is to attain an effective balance of cost and program results.

Benefits in the past grew with the company, and new ones were added only because the company had more money to spend. Planned objectives to benefit programs are vital.

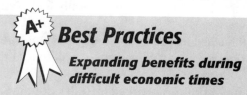

Best Practices

Expanding benefits during difficult economic times

During tough economic times, priorities often change. Perks, such as concierge services, are often viewed as unnecessary expenses that can be cut. However, Pfizer is an example of a company that has actually expanded benefits during tough times. After one year of service, employees now receive three weeks of vacation, where before they had to wait five years. Adoption benefits have been increased from $5,000 to $10,000. And the company now offers a vision plan as part of its health insurance coverage.

(Fortune 100 Best Companies to Work For, How Companies Satisfy Workers, Fortune Magazine, January 20, 2003.)

On what objectives is your benefit program built?

A benefit program can serve the objectives of your company in several ways. The key is for your company to decide on its objectives and then develop programs that will lead to those goals. Too often a company adds a benefit to its program as a result of a manager's reading a magazine article or hearing of a new benefit being offered in the industry. Think about the following example:

Mitsuki, the company's CEO, just walked into HR and announced that a new benefit should be offered to employees. She excitedly related how she read about the new hot benefit of pet insurance in this morning's newspaper and how she thought this would be a perfect benefit to offer. Does this really fit with the company's benefit objectives? Or will the company just waste money and time on another "hot" benefit that employees won't appreciate?

Of course, this—acting impulsively or on a "hot" benefit—is not the best way to modify any benefits program.

Before you determine what to offer in your benefits program, consider the different types of benefits that are generally included in a benefits program.

- ◆ **Insurance.** Types of hazard insurance include pensions, life insurance, termination pay, health insurance, accident and sick and disability.
- ◆ **Paid leaves.** Payment for time not worked includes holidays, vacations, sick leave and rest periods.
- ◆ **Income supplement.** Supplemental income programs include profit sharing, savings plans, credit unions, tuition refunds and discount purchases.
- ◆ **Common services and programs.** Other typical policies and practices that provide a service benefit to the employee include counseling, vanpooling, child care services, relocation reimbursement, parking and cafeteria facilities, training and social and recreation programs.

Benefit objective priorities

Determining what your corporate benefit objectives are is a function of leadership, how you want to be perceived versus your competition, employee security and equality of benefit options. It's essential that benefits be selected based on the objective priorities chosen by your company.

Example 1: *The Leo Company has stated that one of its most important objectives is to recruit the most outstanding employees in the technical fields necessary to produce their product. One way to align employee benefit plans with this objective is to design them with minimal waiting periods for eligibility, early participation and short vesting periods.*

Example 2: *Dion Lyon Incorporated has had trouble with employee turnover and now wants to reduce this problem. One of the ways a benefit program can reduce turnover is for the benefit system to be more progressive in its rewards, with service rewards and penalties for early termination. One key way to motivate employees places an emphasis on incentive provisions.*

Leadership objectives. Leadership objectives refer to a company's desire to be a leader in providing innovative benefits, or at least the leader in a given industry. A leadership objective is not fulfilled simply by "keeping up with the Joneses" in the industry.

A company that is only concerned with what other companies are doing may miss a real opportunity to help its own employees if the demographics or needs of the two employee groups don't match. Statistics need to be tempered by human concerns.

Competitive objectives. Companies may decide to attain a position that is competitive in the benefits area. The attempt is to have comparable and observable elements of the benefit package at a competitive level of prevailing practices.

Some companies copy the prevailing benefits practices in the industry but then cut back funding. Their objective appears to be competitive, but it's difficult to really make a comparison between the benefit systems.

This strategy probably is not serving a competitive objective. In this situation, it may be better to develop a totally different system.

Employee security objectives. Security interests offer employers the best chance for meeting employee benefit concerns. Benefits such as sick pay protect employees' security needs by preventing lost income when employees are unable to work due to illness. The goal is to increase employee "peace of mind."

On a somewhat lesser level, the security aspect of benefits may make the everyday life of employees simpler. The employee knows, for example, that:

◆ He or she has a dependable ride to work through a vanpool;

◆ His or her children are being adequately cared for because of child care services; or

◆ He or she can receive help during a rough time with personal counseling through an EAP, thus being likely to work more efficiently on the job.

Equality in benefit systems. Achieving equality in benefits systems is a goal that can have a company-wide effect on working atmosphere. Equality in benefits tends to create a climate where all employees are treated alike. The feeling promoted is that "We are all in this together," which many of today's flatly structured organizations try to achieve.

Simple examples of this policy include providing the same company-provided health insurance or the same amount of life insurance to all employees, regardless of position. Other examples include not providing preferential parking or private dining rooms for senior management only.

Do your current benefit programs work?

No matter what goals are chosen for a benefits program, the program must be periodically evaluated to determine whether it's meeting both the objectives set by the company and the needs of employees.

You can use a management-by-objectives approach to measure a benefit program. By using this approach, you do a periodic assessment of progress against stated goals. You will also engage in a continuous assessment of your employees' needs through informal interviews and meetings or through formal surveys.

Measuring the relative importance of services to employees and how well current programs are meeting stated needs offers a good indication of whether any revisions to the benefits program are needed. Workforce demographics change constantly, as do employee expectations, legal requirements, competitive pressures and benefit alternatives.

To get the most employee satisfaction and company return on the benefit dollar, the benefits manager must be in tune with the changes in benefit opportunities and the requirements of employees, and be able to adjust to those changes.

No matter what goals are chosen for a benefits and services program, the program must be periodically assessed to determine if it's meeting both the objectives set by the company and the needs of employees. The benefit program can be measured according to a management-by-objectives approach whereby a periodic assessment of progress against stated goals is undertaken. In addition, continuous assessment of employee needs through informal interviews and meetings or formal surveys is necessary.

Measuring the relative importance of services to employees and how well current programs are meeting stated needs offers a good indication of whether any revision is needed. Demographics of the workforce change constantly, as do employee expectations, legal requirements, competitive pressures and alternatives for services to be offered.

The Quiz

1. Employees are much more satisfied with ☐ True ☐ False
   a uniform benefit package because
   everyone gets the same benefits.

2. Which of the following prevents effective communication:
   a. Thinking ahead to frame a reply.
   b. Nonresponsive answers to questions.
   c. Inability to see or hear what is being talked about.
   d. All of the above.

3. A cafeteria-style benefit plan gives employees ☐ True ☐ False
   flexibility in their benefit choices.

4. A high-cost benefit will always be more ☐ True ☐ False
   valued by employees.

5. Why is it important to communicate effectively with employees
   about benefits?
   a. To attract and retain employees.
   b. To be in compliance with laws and regulations.
   c. To protect your financial bottom line.
   d. All of the above.

Answer key: 1.F; 2. d; 3; T; 4. F; 5; d.

Strategic performance management

Martina is the HR director of a large software company. A hot new product is under development and everyone in the company is coping with deadline pressures. Martina notices that several of the managers are months behind in turning in performance reviews on their direct reports to HR. Martina's first instinct is to lecture the managers on the importance of performance management and to threaten them with discipline if their reviews have not been completed by a certain date that Martina picks because it coincides with when HR reports are typically run. What other options could Martina explore?

Start with the business objective

HR strategy involves first identifying business direction and then the people capabilities you need to execute on that direction. A defined performance management strategy is a way to connect the business direction with the people capabilities. Strategic performance management focuses on how to increase employee effectiveness, productivity and shareholder value.

WHAT you need to know

> Most organizations probably view performance management as a way to measure the extent to which an employee's performance meets the requirements of his or her job. But performance management can also be used to align the workforce with the organization's goals, to open communication, and to strengthen the relationship between employer and employee. That can result in positive labor relations and improved retention.

Clearly these goals can't be achieved if performance management is viewed as an annual event that "the top tells the middle to do to the bottom" or as just one more item on the "to do" list. Effective performance management requires that you define and establish performance objectives or goals, that you continuously monitor actual performance, that you provide feedback about how well or poorly employees are doing, and that you implement a fair reward (both positive and negative) system. In short, it requires a solid strategy that is aligned with your company's vision, mission and goals.

Components of performance management

Typical components of a performance management system include:
- performance planning;
- feedback;
- evaluation; and
- development.

Effective performance management combines a performance evaluation or appraisal system with a reward system. Thus, pay and discipline policies would be important components of performance management. An effective disciplinary or pay system is integrated with effective performance review and appraisal. Other reward and recognition policies must also be integrated to form your overall performance management system.

Want to shift your thought patterns to achieve strategic positioning? Here are some of the key ways that traditional HR management differs from strategic HR management:

Traditional: Focus on creating and managing programs.
Strategic: Focus on meeting corporate goals.
Traditional: Compliance.
Strategic: Implementation of strategic initiatives.
Traditional: Employees as customers.
Strategic: Company's business leaders and executives are customers.
Traditional: Cost center.
Strategic: Business partner.

Planning—the first step

The first step in effective performance management is performance planning. Identify your company's business direction—that is, where are you going and how can performance management help you get there? Only after you've selected your destination can you realistically look for the path that will take you there.

Look to your company's business, culture and values. What is important to your company's success and how do your employees help you to achieve that success? The answers will drive your strategy for performance management, both in terms of what competencies are evaluated and the methodology for doing it.

For example, if a company is focused on projecting a professional image, such as a financial services organization, "professional appearance" may be important for an employee who interacts one-on-one with the public. But it may not be important at all for someone working at a computer-help call center where the emphasis is on solving a specified number of customer problems per hour. Or a forced rankings system may not fit the strategy and culture of a team-oriented, entrepreneurial organization because such a system can lead to reduced risk-taking and increased fear of failure.

Identify your company's position on competing priorities—do you want to recognize the team or the individual? Are you results-oriented or does the company place a high value on specific behaviors? Are you looking to identify the best and the brightest or do you want to motivate and retain skilled workers?

Does your company already have a system in place? What is its purpose? Do you know? Do your managers and employees know? If the answers aren't immediately apparent, it may be time to re-evaluate exactly what you hope to accomplish with performance management.

DON'T miss this

"In truth, the performance management system that works for one organization may not produce the same value in another organization," says Colleen O'Neill, Ph.D., who leads Mercer's talent management consulting in the U.S. (Mercer Human Resources Consulting press release, December 17, 2002). "The most powerful solution is specific to an individual organization and is aligned with that organization's unique business and human capital strategy. Putting the right performance management practices in place can produce a significant financial return and an edge that competitors will find difficult to replicate."

What's in it for your company?

What benefits can any employer expect if it invests in a thoughtful performance management system?

WHAT you need to know

The strategic purpose of a performance appraisal system, after all, is to further the employer's business success through employees whose skills are well-matched to the company's objectives, who understand the company's business goals, and who are working effectively towards them.

In most cases, the benefits of a performance evaluation system will include the following:

Consistency. Overall, the selection of employees for promotion, transfer or other action should be more consistent when you're using an effective performance management system. The right person should be matched with the right job more often. This should translate into higher productivity and greater organizational efficiency.

Motivation. All the organization's employees (as well as supervisors and managers) should be more highly motivated. Why? Objective performance appraisal will identify those who are outstanding performers, and management—applying promotion, transfer and other policies—will reward them. Every employee will realize that the organization rewards specific performance that translates into business success, and many employees will be encouraged to improve their performance, thus furthering the company's business goals.

Morale and retention. More highly motivated employees are likely to be more loyal, as well, so that management will have better success retaining valuable employees even as the work force becomes more mobile. Stimulating and reinforcing behaviors that align with the company's purpose and strategy create a sense of belonging, along with higher productivity, better morale, and a more dedicated staff willing to provide the kind of discretionary effort critical to the success of the business.

Organizational impact. Researchers in human behavior stress that individual employees grow in maturity and responsibility if their efforts are accurately evaluated and rewarded. Moreover, if you have a clearly defined organizational direction, with performance objectives for individual employees that cascade down from that direction, you have aligned employees with your mission. People like to work for a company that has a clear meaning and purpose, and you should end up with a more dedicated and responsive employee population. The organization should see daily benefits—including financial—from having more responsible people throughout.

Training needs. While accurate evaluation is most often recommended for its role in making "good employees better," evaluation has a valuable remedial use as well. Effective performance evaluation can identify employees who need training and developmental assistance—and not all of them will be recent hires. Conducting this kind of "gap analysis" on a regular basis will identify recruiting and training requirements as well as provide a more accurate prediction of whether existing employees can carry out the organization's business plan.

Reduce termination risks. Employees who are so sufficiently weak that they should be dismissed can be spotted with more certainty under an evaluation system. Perhaps more importantly, management may be more willing to dismiss an inadequate employee if an objective evaluation system can be pointed to as identifying the inadequacy. Both employees and the organization should benefit from an early end to a bad situation.

Motivated, engaged employees are more productive

Traditional performance management is designed to tell management who is performing, who is not, who might be suitable for another assignment, and who is a candidate for promotion. But some performance management systems take on a larger, strategic role: they are designed to *motivate and align the workforce with the organization's business objectives.*

Accepting that performance appraisal systems can be designed to motivate and influence the individual employee, here are examples of the higher productivity that can be expected:

1. An employee who understands the business goals and is highly motivated will, without management's help, find new innovations and efficiencies.
2. A motivated and self-directed employee will build a quality focus into his or her work, increasing operating efficiency and reducing costs.
3. Engaged and motivated employees give more discretionary effort.
4. Employees who are motivated by the business goals have a sense of control over the details of their work and will see

the larger picture. Armed with knowledge of the business and the role they play in it, they may be able to identify new opportunities or competitive threats more quickly and accurately, thus contributing to the organization's ability to change to meet business realities.

Connection to employee commitment

Effective performance management has a strong connection to employee commitment, satisfaction and engagement. Those qualities, in turn, affect important business outcomes such as turnover and productivity.

WHAT you need to know

Mercer Human Resource Consulting, in its 2002 "People at Work" survey (press release dated February 5, 2003), looked at the connection between employee attitudes about performance management and commitment and satisfaction:

◆ Among employees who said they'd had a formal performance appraisal in the last 12 months, 62 percent expressed a strong sense of commitment to their organization. This compares to 49 percent for employees who had not had a formal performance appraisal during the past 12 months.

◆ Among employees who are coached by their manager, 80 percent feel a strong sense of commitment to the organization, compared to 46 percent among employees who are not coached.

◆ Among employees who say they have clearly defined performance goals, only 18 percent are seriously thinking about leaving their organization, while among those without clearly defined goals, 46 percent are thinking of leaving. Likewise, employees who don't understand how their performance is evaluated are more likely to be thinking about leaving (18 percent vs. 41 percent).

◆ Among employees who say good performance is recognized, 81 percent express overall satisfaction with their organization, compared to 37 percent for those who say good performance is not recognized. Similarly, employees who say good performance is rewarded express higher satisfaction than employees who say good performance is not rewarded (88 percent vs. 47 percent).

Organizational factors that influence performance systems

Many factors go into the decision of whether to adopt a formal performance management system. The most important factor, however, is how a performance management system can contribute to your organization's overall success—whether by enhancing the bottom line through productivity gains, increasing retention of desirable employees, or avoiding such productivity drains as low morale, complaints and grievances, or even litigation.

Size of staff

Size is a primary factor in deciding whether to adopt a formal performance appraisal policy and how detailed the system must be. The "traditional" rule of thumb is that a single manager can follow the careers of 12 to 15 subordinates; of course, this rule of thumb doesn't take into consideration the complexity of the workplace, impacts of globalization or technology, telecommuting or the difficulty in recruiting and retaining staff.

WHAT you need to know

> Ask yourself whether a more formalized performance appraisal system will support your business' strategic goals. Will the cost of change or implementing a new process be justified by improved performance? How will you quantify that? Or is the informal system that you use currently sufficient to support your company's business goals? The economics of the operation simply may not support nor require a more complex employer-employee relationship.

Compliance

Equal employment opportunity laws require that race, sex, age, national origin and other listed factors not be used as a basis for employment decisions. An efficient way to assure that supervisors and managers don't use those factors in evaluating employees may be to dictate the rating factors that will be used.

You don't want your performance appraisals to form the basis of a lawsuit. Even a well-designed system can open you up to liability if it's poorly implemented or applied inconsistently. You want to be as consistent and fair as possible. And if your performance appraisals are legally questionable, they're probably flawed enough to drive employees away as well.

✓ Checklist

Appraise without fear

- ☐ Use the test of "business necessity" — evaluate only those areas that are necessary for effective job performance.
- ☐ Maintain accurate, up-to-date job descriptions.
- ☐ Communicate clear job standards so employees understand what they need to do to get top ratings in their appraisals.
- ☐ Don't allow performance problems to continue unchecked; document problems as they arise so you can reference these records in your appraisal preparations.
- ☐ Be aware that outside forces (family or health problems) may be a contributing factor for poor performers. While you should be aware of such issues, and perhaps help with an accommodation or a referral to an EAP, you cannot allow them to justify poor performance. Be careful, though, not to run afoul of leave and disability laws.
- ☐ Make performance evaluation an ongoing process and have appraisals filed correctly for employee reference.
- ☐ Work to establish an organization culture in which top managers support their peers' efforts to discipline poor performers.
- ☐ Be open to the possibility that an employee may not be in the position that best suits his or her abilities; you might consider rotating employees into different jobs. A terrible customer service rep who's not a "people person" might be a whiz at overhauling your filing system.

Internal inconsistencies

Sometimes internal politics will lead management to adopt a system, as opposed to continuing an informal practice. Employee discontent over individual managers' ratings—even though management may agree with the ratings—might be resolved by setting up a formal system that presumably will have greater credibility.

Control

Strategic employers realize the value of employee resources. Even so, for many employers, people costs are the largest single line item on a balance sheet. Therefore, to properly manage both the value of human capital and account for, audit and report on this critical resource, some system of evaluation must exist.

> **Example:** As employees work cross-functionally across time zones and in many diverse geographic locations, a manager may find herself supervising people in three different professions in three different locations. Left to her own performance appraisal devices, that manager might tentatively generalize that "Smith seems dedicated; Jones is impressive. The others are doing all right." For expensive assets such as three professional employees, this is a very simplistic and risky method of management.

Steps for performance appraisal design

Based on your understanding of the business needs and purposes, what do you do if you have decided that it makes sense strategically to implement a performance appraisal system? Or, if you already have a system in place, what if you want to improve it so it better supports the business goals and objectives? Although designing a performance appraisal system is beyond the scope of this book, a number of steps in the process must align with your organization's business purposes for your appraisal process to be effective.

✔ ✔ Checklist

Performance appraisal design steps

Below are fourteen sequential design steps you can follow to create your own system or audit an existing one. The steps highlighted in boldface type are discussed further, as they are most critical for aligning your performance management approach with your business strategy.

- ☐ **Define purpose, objectives and strategy.**
- ☐ **Conduct or review job analysis.**
- ☐ **Obtain employee input and feedback.**
- ☐ Review standards for objectivity.
- ☐ Design a standardized method of appraisal.
- ☐ Develop documentation.
- ☐ Conduct initial management training.
- ☐ Conduct employee training.
- ☐ Incorporate independent performance monitors.
- ☐ **Communicate results.**
- ☐ **Provide continuing resources as needed.**
- ☐ Support your supervisors.
- ☐ **Audit, evaluate and report periodically.**
- ☐ **Continue benchmarking and study.**

Define purpose, objectives and strategy

Your first step is to clearly state the purpose of the system. Solicit input throughout the organization to get support and consensus for that purpose. Your performance management system must result in an alignment between the competencies and behaviors on which employees are evaluated (and rewarded) and the overall success factors for your business.

To create this kind of alignment, consider establishing a task force of managers and supervisors initially; however, include line employees at an early point in the process.

DON'T
miss
this

Listen carefully to what line managers, in particular, identify as factors in successful performance. Contrast that with what senior leadership sees as critical skills to move the business forward. Are there any gaps? Are the two perspectives in alignment? How can you identify competencies or evaluation strategies to bridge that gap or to sharpen the performance focus?

Other planning strategies include:

◆ Benchmark competitors and industry leaders.
◆ Determine whether or not a consultant should be employed. If yes, design a project budget and controls before interviewing candidates.
◆ Appoint a project manager and create time lines whether or not a consultant is used.
◆ Establish accountability.

Conduct or review job analysis

What are the elements of each job to be evaluated? The type of information needed for an appraisal system will vary from employer to employer depending upon the business, the jobs to be analyzed and the objectives of the system.

Example: *Is a customer service representative expected to spot and correct errors in a customer's account, or simply to input accurately new material from the customer? Is courtesy an element of the representative's job? How much time should be devoted to courtesy as opposed to answering the waiting call? How is that measured? How does the CSR's job support the overall business strategy? Would changes in the job description more accurately reflect expectations necessary to grow the business? Is a new emphasis on customer service part of the business strategy? What specific behaviors reflect improved customer service?*

Most performance appraisal systems consider at least some of the following factors:

- Work quality parameters, such as customer satisfaction, error rates and complaint data, among others.
- Measurement units.
- Production standards.
- Existing reporting systems.

After each job has been analyzed, it must be described. If the job is described in terms of its economic value to the employer, then it may have to be redescribed in terms of the human skills and effort required to perform it.

> **Example:** *A security guard's job may be to "check the identification of anyone entering or leaving, allow no wrapped parcels to pass in or out, and generally protect the premises during off-shift hours." The skills to perform that job, however, may begin with proficiency in using firearms, if the guard is to be armed. The effort required might include keeping a rigid checkpoint schedule; or it may involve telling valued customers—tactfully—that they will have to return during normal business hours. These are the factors that the employer will list when it describes the guard job in terms of what it takes to perform it.*

Again, it cannot be stressed too strongly that it's necessary to develop a thorough analysis and understanding of the employees' duties to be evaluated. By its nature, performance appraisals cannot be implemented without such analysis.

> **Example:** *A mechanic in a repair shop may have a single demand made upon him: diagnose problems discovered by others and repair them correctly the first time. If that is, in fact, what is being asked of the mechanic, then only performance testing would appear to hold much promise as an evaluation method.*
>
> *Observation of the employee ("he seems to know what he is doing") and statements by others might contribute little and could actually produce irrelevant judgments that unjustifiably weigh the evaluation for or against the employee. A personality test may be pointless if all that is wanted is competent mechanical work, and interface appraisals may be irrelevant if the mechanic has virtually no contact with people.*

Obtain employee input and feedback

Review the job standards with all employee groups, from senior management to entry level. Seek input and revision. What doesn't make sense? What standards are unspoken, or are established but ignored? How is success really defined? Review each challenge with line management.

WHAT you need to know

> By discussing the criteria *before* the system begins, you'll avoid errors and develop a system in which everyone feels ownership. More importantly, you'll be evaluating performance based on factors that actually support the business objectives and strategy. Plus, the more ownership people have, the less resistance there will be when the system is implemented.

Without clearly defined uniform standards in ranking, supervisors and managers will use standards of their own that may, or may not, be valid—and that will undoubtedly be inconsistent across the organization. Also, the less consistent standards are, the more likely employees will be to feel they're being treated unfairly.

Remember Martina's problem with untimely performance appraisals? One strategy would be to look into the way that the performance appraisal system is structured. Does it place unreasonable technical and time requirements on managers or other evaluators? Regardless of how comprehensive or elegantly designed, a system that includes too many attributes or that takes an inordinate amount of time to complete will be devalued by managers, who either won't do appraisals at all or who will find ways to subvert the process in order to save time. If the current system is complicated and inordinately time-consuming, Martina may be better off crafting something relatively straightforward.

When an HR department focuses solely on compliance or on the few managers that "aren't behaving," it isn't acting strategically. Instead, HR's credibility shrinks in the eyes of those managers that are trying to grow the business. Good managers want to use HR in leveraging a company's human capital to grow the business. According to Joseph A. Wert, Senior Vice President and National Practice Leader for the human resources innovation practice of The Segal Company, if HR is more focused on serving as "internal police" than on understanding the business' goals and helping managers achieve them, managers won't turn to HR for an entrepreneurial business partnership.

If the existing appraisal system is not inordinately time-consuming, Martina could examine the company's performance management system for managers. What are the managers being evaluated on? Is timely performance appraisal one of their deliverables? If not, it shouldn't be surprising that the managers' attention is focused elsewhere.

Finally, Martina could examine the objectives of her company's performance management system. She may be surprised to find that the employees are meeting those objectives despite the lack of annual performance reviews. Martina may want to consider doing away with them and relying on a system of ongoing appraisal that may be what is happening in practice anyway.

The design of instructions, evaluation forms and questionnaires has a lot to do with the accuracy of "traditional" evaluation, the kind of evaluation designed to tell management who is performing, who is not, who might be suitable for transfer, and who is a candidate for promotion. But what about evaluations designed to *motivate?* That is, if the performance appraisal is used as the occasion for an employee's evaluation of his own performance and for setting new short-term goals for the coming evaluation period, does "accuracy" matter? Of course it matters! Performance appraisals are official company records. These records can form the basis of a company's defense. Of greater impact, these records document the value of an employee to the organization.

Provide resources as needed

It would be strategically silly to invest the time and effort necessary to establish a performance system aligned with the company's business objectives and then fail to support it adequately. Performance appraisal systems work best in the context of a supportive organizational structure. Support your performance appraisal system with:

◆ Communication skills training for conflict situations and appeals;

◆ Counseling resources, including employee assistance programs (EAPs);

◆ Orientation programs that include an explanation of the performance appraisal program;

◆ Articles in company newsletters; and

◆ Explanations in employee handbooks.

Audit, evaluate and report periodically

Is your performance appraisal system accomplishing what you wanted it to? The value of a performance management system can and should be calculated in monetary terms. Consider the cost of designing, implementing and performing the appraisal weighed against the returns.

WHAT you need to know

There should be tangible evidence linking the purpose of the system with its results. This is an often-neglected step in the performance appraisal process.

Here are some factors to consider:

◆ Are error rates lower?

◆ Is turnover reduced?

◆ Have customer complaints decreased?

◆ Is new product development more efficient and effective?

◆ Are budgets more accurate?

◆ Has profitability per employee increased?

◆ Has market penetration increased?

◆ Have cycle times decreased?

If the system is not achieving its purposes, identify the trouble spots and address them. This may require you to rethink the process (in whole or in part). But remember, continuous improvement is what you seek, and reevaluation is not necessarily a bad result.

Make certain that you report the results periodically to senior management. Be sure to audit the system for compliance issues and stereotypical assumptions, as well as for how well the system supports your business goals. Be proactive.

Continue benchmarking and study

Stay current with new performance appraisal trends and theories. Identify where they may be applicable to your organizational environment. Technology is continually improving in its ability to track, analyze and forecast workplace data. Evaluating the data your performance appraisal system yields can identify knowledge and skill gaps, pinpoint critical competencies, isolate pockets of excellence that can then be reinforced and duplicated, and highlight high as well as low performers—all information that can prove of strategic value in moving the business forward, faster and more profitably.

The big picture—evaluation plus rewards

Performance appraisals are primarily a policy that serves other policies, all of which should "roll up" to serve the overall business success. Many policies affecting the employment relationship can be implemented without making changes in other policies. Flexible working hours, for example, can be set up to meet child-care, commuting or other employee needs without making major changes in most personnel and payroll policies or practices.

Employee evaluation, however, is for the most part pointless unless it's closely tied to the business' overall strategy, plus several other policies, to form an overall performance management system.

Employers who want to encourage their employees to contribute fully towards business success will need an accurate evaluation system as step one of that process, and a system of rewards as step two. The rewards may include promotions and transfers, new assignments, as well as incentive and merit pay increases. Formal and informal recognition on a daily basis can be a major part of any rewards system.

Deliberate policies, however, are necessary for any of this to happen in an organization of any size.

Policy versus practice

In most companies, employers who have performance evaluation systems generally require their supervisors and managers to apply set criteria or standards in evaluating each employee.

The key to making performance management systems more strategic is the degree to which the performance management system is aligned with and supports the overall business strategy.

In contrast, the employer with a system or policy that is not tied concretely to the organization's business objectives may result in evaluating employees on whatever criteria the HR department thinks appropriate. This may or may not support the overall business goals.

Does it matter whether an employee is evaluated with the help of a performance system that is based on organizational success factors—or because he or she was the manager's choice for whatever reason?

Example: *Nigel's employer uses a performance appraisal system that evaluates all employees using the same competencies. Nigel, a member of the organization's research and development team, consistently receives high marks on his evaluations. When senior leadership comes looking for someone to head up a new product development initiative that they've determined is critical for business success, they look to Nigel because he has been rated so highly. However, under Nigel's leadership the initiative stalls; after months of meetings nearly nothing has been accomplished.*

Upon closer examination, it becomes apparent that Nigel's high ratings are based on competencies such as punctuality, product knowledge and detail-orientation, not innovation, creativity or project management. This is a classic example of performance criteria that is not particularly aligned with business strategy.

Best Practices

Ongoing appraisals replace annual performance reviews

When Bristol-Myers Squibb was using a 360-degree, paper-and-pencil traditional performance appraisal system, no one was satisfied with the results. The system was inordinately time-consuming and focused on what employees had already done, not on goals and growth. With Bristol-Myers' 44,000 employees affected, even the head of leadership development at the company called it "nightmarish."

In "Better Performance Reviews, Great Results," *Workforce Management*, November 2001, author Janet Wiscombe tells how the company hired an HR consulting firm to help it design its approach. Rather than conducting annual performance "marathons," Bristol-Myers' new program concentrates on ongoing appraisals. It uses immediate feedback and coaching, along with clarified and significantly raised standards, to focus on future expectations. Moreover, the system removes passivity from the employee performance appraisal experience. Employees are accountable to ask for feedback and are given ongoing support and training to achieve their potential.

Notably, involuntary terminations at the company increased by 25 percent over the past five years, largely because standards were raised. (Remember that not all retention is good retention.) The company's leadership believes that the new system is directly related to the company's business success.

Alternatives to traditional appraisals

Several alternatives or modifications to traditional performance appraisal programs are available to organizations that want to try something else. With the increasing emphasis on teamwork, shared decision-making, and innovation, the old evaluation approach based on a top-down ranking and tied to a raise may no longer fit your needs.

De-couple the performance appraisal components

Tom Coens and Mary Jenkins have written a book titled: *Abolishing Performance Appraisals: Why They Backfire And What to do Instead* (Berrett-Koehler, December 2000). But they don't advocate abolishing goal-setting, coaching or measuring results. Instead, one approach they discuss is to "de-couple" everything that is included in the typical review: coaching, feedback, compensation and promotion decisions and legal documentation.

Treating these as separate processes, and designing programs accordingly, can help tailor the processes to better meet individual and organizational goals. Many successful organizations have found that continuous assessment and feedback, tied to the business cycle, is much more effective in achieving results than the annual performance review process.

Change assessment cycle to reflect business reality

Another approach is simply to move away from annual performance management to project-based performance management. Instead of always basing a review on a hire date, it makes more sense to synchronize it with the organization's business cycle. So, for example, if your organization's overreaching goal is to support new product and new business development, tie the timing of your performance evaluations to specific new product or new business development projects.

DON'T miss this

Timing for evaluations may be at specific project milestones or at the conclusion of the project. It makes sense to employees and management alike to evaluate progress towards their goals against the business results they've achieved.

Or, you could tie compensation and promotion decisions to the organization's budget cycle. Making compensation and promotion decisions after 4th quarter results are available serves to correlate individual performance directly to business results.

Change process from top-down to bottom-up

Want to create ownership, engagement and a sense of empowerment in your employees? Make your performance management system one that is initiated by the employees, who evaluate their own performance against jointly developed goals and pre-established competencies, and then seek feedback, coaching and development from their managers.

WHAT you need to know

Employee-initiated performance management changes the perception of the manager being accountable for the employee's performance to the employee being accountable for the employee's performance. Employee-initiated development and performance assessment builds employee initiative and ownership—which in turn aids your efforts to support the organization's business success.

✓ ✓ ✓ Checklist

Ten ways to get better performance management results

While there may be no "silver bullet" or quick fix for enhancing performance management, you can take specific steps to maximize its effectiveness. Mercer's research and its consulting experience with top performing companies indicate that the following ten design principles will lead to better results (Mercer Human Resources Consulting's Knowledge Center, April 1, 2003).

1. **Reflect your company's performance values.** Your company's underlying priorities should guide decisions about performance. The performance management process should reinforce the messages that the organization wants to send about its business, talent, performance, rewards, advancement and careers. Those values should be clearly communicated.

2. **Get commitment and active participation of executives.** Never underestimate the power of the executive team's words and behaviors—executives can set an example and build commitment for effective performance management in leaders at all levels. The more you can actively engage leaders at all levels in the process, the more successful performance management will be.

3. **Focus on the "right" performance measures.** The key purpose of performance management is to focus people on doing the right things. Align your employee performance model with your company's business model and focus on the "mission-critical" performance measures. Spend time ensuring a common performance vocabulary and a calibrated sense of performance success among leaders at all levels; calibration ensures a consistent success profile and produces consistent results between raters.

4. **Hold managers accountable for performance feedback and differentiation.** Managers will be motivated to conduct valid appraisals when they are given the skills and tools to collect valid performance data and when they are held accountable, through appropriate measurement and feedback, for making valid performance decisions.

5. **Establish complementary roles and responsibilities.** Take steps to ensure employees and managers share accountability for performance management. Expect managers to "own" the outcomes and HR to "own" the process.

6. **Integrate with other business and human resource processes.** Synchronize business and individual performance management cycles. Align business planning with goal setting for individuals and teams. Integrate talent acquisition, talent development, performance management and rewards systems. Talent management processes should reinforce the same mes-

sages about performance excellence. Clearly define the link between performance and pay.

7. **Minimize administrative burden.** Leveraging available technology can minimize the administrative burden and maximize participation and support. But don't just automate an overly complicated process. Look for opportunities to streamline your process steps and simplify administrative requirements.

8. **Provide necessary communication and training.** Enhance performance management "skill" and "will." Training should enhance the range of required performance management skills, as well as the reasons to do performance management well. Make sure that managers understand the financial return that high performance management practices generate. Teach all stakeholders the necessary skills and support the process through ongoing communication.

9. **Measure and track success.** The right metrics will allow you to track the success of your performance management practices. An assessment of the business impact can help to prioritize performance management activities. Analyze what people say, but also what they do. The "true" performance management system can be considerably different than the system perceived to be in place.

10. **Engage in continuous improvement.** Performance management is an ongoing process that should reflect the current and emerging business challenges, as well as the company's values about performance and careers. As the business and workforce change, modify the performance management process. Ensure that the performance management process and tools remain congruent with organizational values and priorities. But resist the temptation to change everything every year.

The Quiz

1. A performance management system that works for one organization will always produce the same value in another organization.   ❏ True   ❏ False

2. Which of the following is not a component of performance management?
   a. performance planning
   b. feedback
   c. evaluation
   d. development
   e. pay policy
   f. disciplinary system
   g. flexible hours

3. Effective performance appraisal systems need not be complex or overly time-consuming for supervisors.   ❏ True   ❏ False

4. The value of a performance management system can be calculated in monetary terms.   ❏ True   ❏ False

5. Having the same competencies to be evaluated across the entire organization ensures consistency; there is no need to tailor competencies to specific jobs.   ❏ True   ❏ False

Answer key: 1. F; 2. g; 3. T; 4. T; 5. F.

Strategic training & development

The R&D department at Delia's company has discovered a way to make light bulbs that last five years but cost the same as those that currently last only 1200 hours. The company wants to ramp-up production of these miracle bulbs quickly before the market is flooded with similar items.

All company resources are being focused on this new product and on becoming the leader in the long-life bulb business. How will Delia, the head of the company's training team, help the company attain its goal?

How training helps meet strategic goals

Training, in its most basic sense, gives an employee the information necessary to perform a task proficiently. If orientation gives employees a sense of a company's goals, training provides the tools to achieve those goals.

WHAT you need to know

> The fundamental purposes of training program design is to assimilate employees into the workplace; "educate and reeducate" employees about the workplace, the company's goals and objectives, how their jobs fit into those goals and objectives, and how to perform their jobs; and to provide personal development programs.

Training falls into three general categories:

◆ **Technical training** is teaching an employee how to perform specific tasks (computer training, customer service training).
◆ **Development training** can include development aspects (supervisory training or management training).
◆ **Personal training** provides individual skills such as conflict resolution training or time management training.

But in each case, the objective is to focus the employee's skills or mindset on meeting the company's strategic plan.

✔ ✔ *Checklist*

Types of training programs

Training programs (formal and informal) may be:

☐ *Executive development programs*—leadership, strategic planning, policy and decision making, crisis handling, financial management and change management;
☐ *Management and supervisory development*—motivation theory, workplace attitudes, group dynamics, goal setting, team building, delegation and grievance procedures;
☐ *Professional development*—technology and related management applications;

- ☐ *Organizational development*—transition workshops, change-management strategies, behavior modeling, conflict resolution and creative problem solving;
- ☐ *Skills and technical training*—entry-level, remedial, upgrading, retraining, cross-training and reentry training programs;
- ☐ *Orientation programs*—new employee, update programs and modified orientation for rehires;
- ☐ *Computer and related training*—overview, systems, hardware, software, communications and security;
- ☐ *Specific company-needed training*—safety, communications, diversity and intercultural programs, foreign language, new product/methods and procedures, assertiveness and adventure (outdoor) programs;
- ☐ *Behavior management*—ethics, personal growth, stress management, wellness, employee/labor relations and sensitivity training programs;
- ☐ *Customer service*—customer relations, customer service and cross-selling;
- ☐ *Sales training*—product features, sourcing, vendor relations and marketing;
- ☐ *Basic education*—literacy and proficiency; and
- ☐ *Informal training programs*—on-the-job programs, coaching, job rotation and participation in community groups.

Advantages of training. Among the benefits a company can gain from successful training are:

- ◆ Improved employee performance, including increased quality and quantity of output;
- ◆ A work force ready to step into jobs created by internal changes;
- ◆ Promotable employees to fill vacant positions;
- ◆ Improved employee attitudes and morale, leading to reduced absenteeism and turnover and increased customer satisfaction;
- ◆ Reduction in waste, spoilage and inefficient practices; and
- ◆ Fewer accidents.

Objectives of training programs. Companies train their employees to modify behavior to help achieve the companies' objectives. Be sure that you match training programs to company needs.

DON'T
miss
this

Many trainers get caught in an activity trap. They become so enmeshed in the training offerings that they lose sight of the purpose of the training—to help achieve the company's objectives.

To determine whether specific training is needed, a company should do a performance audit based on its business requirements and organizational goals. Identify major problems and determine whether they're attributable to organizational problems or an employee's inability to do a job. If the employee simply does not possess the skills to do the job adequately, training is appropriate.

In addition, most companies have a need for some sort of training due to the rapid rate of change in technology and public tastes—to keep up with these changes as an organization. Training is also a way to increase productivity and, therefore, the company's bottom line, by improving performance.

Remember Delia from our opening scenario? Here's how she used training to tackle the new light bulb campaign: By setting up a series of training classes. One to communicate the company's plan to all employees. Another to train them to use the new equipment that produces the miracle bulbs. And a third to train the customer service group to use the product so they can help customers with questions.

At the same time, she set up a series of all-employee training sessions to deal with any necessary culture change—for those employees feeling a sense of urgency or a lack of resources when faced with working on both the new bulbs and the old product, and for concerns employees had about the quality of the current products during the new bulb ramp-up.

Delia's approach will help align the employees of the company with its overriding goal—getting up to speed and ready to promote this new product in the marketplace.

Training is not only important for meeting organizational goals and making employees more productive—it can help protect an organization against lawsuits by showing the company's intent.

Worst case scenario

Elian is on the witness stand. He is the defendant in a sexual harassment lawsuit brought against his employer by a customer. The prosecutor just asked Elian if he'd ever had sexual harassment training at work. "Well, not that I recall," is his answer.

When the verdict is read, the company is responsible for paying the customer $15,000,000. Later it comes out that the jurors felt the company did nothing to prevent sexual harassment in its workplace, as evidenced by its lack of sexual harassment prevention training.

Solution: Having a sexual harassment prevention training program shows that the employer wants to prevent sexual harassment in its workplace and wants to protect its customers. It also may work to prevent just that type of behavior and stop expensive lawsuits before they begin.

It is well established that employers can be sued for the actions of an employee acting on behalf of the employer—and if failure to properly train the employee results in harm to a customer or some other individual outside the organization, the employer can be held liable.

WHAT you need to know

> Use training to protect your company's interests.

Developing strategic training programs

"Training" versus "development?" What is the difference? Experts make a distinction between "training," which generally is more focused and oriented toward shorter-term business goals, and "development," which is typically characteristic of programs that provide learning for future opportunities.

Training should be conceptualized and designed as a system to maximize effectiveness—get the company's objectives across "loud and clear." This approach includes defining each step and assigning clear accountabilities.

As a general rule, every training program should be:

◆ Carefully designed for specific purposes;

◆ Developed according to company standards;

◆ Validated to ensure that there is no bias and that the program's content is in fact communicated;

◆ Measurable and tracked against the established criteria, including cost data;

◆ Conducted in a structured and supportive environment; and

◆ Have a beginning and an end.

Best Practices

How to build a strategic training program

According to William R. Tracey, author of *Designing Training and Development Systems* (AMACOM, 1992), several basic principles should govern training program design. The program should be:

◆ **Supported.** Each program must have executive, management and union, if applicable, commitment and support.

◆ **Appropriate.** Training programs address deficiencies in knowledge, skill and attitudes. Training programs cannot resolve performance deficiencies that are caused by improper standards, inadequate supervision, lack of commitment, poor working conditions or other similar work situations.

◆ **Justified.** Programs must address company and employee needs, address all types and levels of staff and service the entire organization.

◆ **Customized.** Training philosophy and curriculum must reflect company culture and values, be organized, address company needs, be flexible and be responsive.

◆ **Systematic.** Training programs must be based on job needs, developed in a systemic manner and use structured materials based on valid learning theory.

- ◆ **Measured.** Training programs must use delivery systems that are effective, utilize appropriate technology, be cost-effective and produce satisfactory results.
- ◆ **Validated.** Training programs must be validated before full implementation.
- ◆ **Evaluated.** All training programs should be evaluated and provide for feedback.
- ◆ **Creditable.** Accepted adult learning theory must be the basis for every program. Participants must be included in needs assessment, planning, implementation and evaluating personal progress and achievement.
- ◆ **Participatory.** Each program should provide every participant with the opportunity to participate and to apply program content.

Knowing how adults learn is critical to the design of training programs. You will not achieve the objectives—strategic or otherwise—you're going after if the training is not successful. To maximize your goal of supporting company strategy, the following learning principles should be incorporated into training program design:

- ◆ The goals of training should be clear to the participants.
- ◆ New material should be related to known material, and each experience should be built upon previous ones. This structure facilitates absorbing the new material into an integrated whole.
- ◆ We learn by watching; thus, modeling is a very valuable technique. Demonstrations, diagrams, videos and pictures are examples of ways in which modeling can be used in training.
- ◆ Because employees learn at different rates, it's important that training participants be screened. If possible, training programs should try to account for differences by variety in presentation formats.
- ◆ Repetition increases learning. Therefore, training courses should include practice of new skills. The more realistic the exercises, the more the concepts will be likely to be accepted, adopted and subsequently used in the workplace.
- ◆ Break tasks into the smallest step. Teach each step sequentially.

- ◆ Space the timing of training sessions. Humans don't have unlimited attention and retention spans. There are exceptions, but as a general rule, it's best to limit the length of each session and offer multiple sessions over time.
- ◆ The majority of trainees will have plateaus in the learning process. Research shows that humans don't absorb knowledge in a steady and unbroken "stream." We absorb new information for a period of time, then we stop learning for a period of time and then we begin learning again.
- ◆ Rewards and reinforcement are important motivators to learning. It may be impossible to separate rewards from feedback (reinforcement).

Evaluating a strategic training program

When evaluating training, you must, of course, consider its cost to the organization. Ask whether the amount of money spent brought about the desired results or if another method should be employed. While cost may not be the only evaluation tool, it's certainly one of the methods that must be used. Tie other evaluations with cost data and compile each.

WHAT you need to know

Design the evaluation instruments first. As part of the design of a training program, build in an evaluation method to assure that the training accomplishes its strategic objective. Evaluation should be an integral part of the training system from the beginning, not an afterthought. It will tell you whether the training has "paid off." In fact, all of the evaluation methods should be established before the actual program is designed to ensure that the evaluation devices are not skewed by the content or the biases of the designers.

Testing and measurement. The testing and measurement of learning are complex subjects. It often requires the expertise of educators, psychologists and statisticians to design and implement measurement methods that meet standards of validity and reliability.

Even without a formal validation, measuring results can provide a good indication of whether a training program has worked. A program can be judged on several levels and with a number of criteria that measure change:

Participant reaction. Asking trainees how they feel about their training and what they think they've gained from it is a relatively limited form of evaluation, although it can be useful.

Why is it limited? In the first place, you may have difficulty getting an honest reaction. Just as in universities where students are asked to evaluate professors and courses, employees will often say "nice things" because they don't want to hurt your feelings or hurt anybody's career. The more specific questions you ask, however, the more likely you are to get usable information about the trainees' reactions.

Even if trainees are honest with you, they may well think they've learned more than they have. They may have really loved the course and learned very little. Because of a positive attitude planted by a talented instructor, they may simply have a good feeling about the experience that has no relation to later job performance. They may feel good because they were selected for a special program or just because someone took the time to notice them.

Participant reaction, of course, won't be all positive. Some trainees will tell you that they found the training a waste of time. Their reactions, too, may be based on many things other than what they did or didn't learn. They may result from a proverbial chip on the shoulder or a general suspicion of anything management does. If you do get a large number of negative reactions, that is a clear signal that there is something wrong with your program or your instructor. Again, ask specific questions that require specific answers.

Examples of some of the more effective questions you can ask participants are:

◆ *What did you learn?*
◆ *What was the most helpful part of the course?*
◆ *What was the least helpful part of the course?*
◆ *How could the instructor have been more effective?*
◆ *Was enough time dedicated to each subject? If not, what would you recommend we change for future programs?*
◆ *How will you apply what you learned in this course when you return to your job?*
◆ *Is there any follow-up training or assistance that you feel might help you implement what you've learned? If yes, what would you recommend?*

Delayed evaluation. Some organizations find it helpful to have participants evaluate a course after they return to their jobs and attempt to put their learning into practice. This method may show how effective the program really is. For example:

◆ If employees feel that more time should have been spent on a particular subject, or that what was learned is inconsistent with how things are really done, changes can be made in the course.

◆ If trainees feel that some sort of follow-up would be helpful, it can then be arranged.

◆ If employees can't remember what they learned, then maybe the participants didn't have an opportunity to apply the training concepts on the job.

Another benefit of waiting to solicit employees' reactions to a course they've attended is that it is often more honest because the instructor isn't present when the form is completed, and their responses are more likely to reflect the value of the course material instead of their personal feelings about the instructor or other biases.

Learning—interior changes. Another gauge of training success is to measure what has actually been learned by the individuals as a direct result of training. A written test or an observation of sample work can tell you whether the information your instructors tried to teach was learned.

Off-the-job learning doesn't necessarily translate into desired on-the-job behavior. However, if the trainees haven't learned the training material, it won't be transferred to the job. It's always a good idea to find out whether learning has occurred.

On-the-job performance. In educational theory, the behavioral objective is the byword. Using a behavioral approach, the trainer begins the program with a very specific list of behavior (not attitude or knowledge) objectives—changes in the trainee's behavior that the training is supposed to bring about. After all, a new attitude toward safety or knowing how to assemble a new product means nothing unless they pay off as productive on-the-job performance.

In deciding whether training has been successful on this level, the production records of those who have received training can be compared with those who have not received training. Do those who undergo training reach an acceptable level of production sooner than others? Do they waste less material, have fewer accidents, file more letters or sell more computers?

Checking on behavior changes six months or a year after the end of a training program will indicate how well the program "took." Have the initial changes faded with time or has the work environment reinforced the new behavior and encouraged its continuance?

Some on-the-job changes in behavior will be difficult to measure, particularly the complex behaviors of supervisors and managers. Interviewing peers, subordinates and supervisors about any detected changes and observing the newly trained manager at work should give an indication of whether the person is putting the training to work.

Organizational changes. Where the effectiveness of training matters the most is how it pays off for the organization as a whole. Various company records will show whether, overall, the training program has had a positive impact, such as:

- Amount and quality of production;
- Materials wasted;
- Number of accidents;
- Clearing out of backlogs;
- Number of grievances;
- Turnover;
- Absenteeism; and
- Sales rates and other business measures.

Management's role. Management plays a key role in the success or failure of any training program. Since training generally occurs as a result of an organizational need for enhanced knowledge and skills, it would seem a foregone conclusion that management would support such an effort. This is usually the case at the senior management level; however, middle managers and first-line supervisors often have mixed feelings about training.

While mid- and first-line managers may agree with the need for employees to upgrade their skills, they are often dismayed at the prospect of employees spending time away from their jobs to attend courses. Furthermore, they often have little or no exposure to the training programs themselves, so they are unable to coach employees to apply what they've learned when they return to the job.

This creates a cycle of failure for the training function: employees who have been trained receive no reinforcement when they attempt to implement new ways of doing things, so the transfer of learning does not take place. Managers and supervisors then conclude that training has no value, since no behavior change occurs as a result of attending a program. Because training is perceived by managers and supervisors as providing no payoff for the organization, they become less likely to permit employees to participate in future programs.

WHAT you need to know

How can a company break this cycle? The first step is to involve middle managers and first-line supervisors in developing training. This has two benefits:

First, it gives managers an opportunity to provide input into the course material, resulting in a program that is more focused and more representative of the "real world."

Second, it allows managers to become familiar with the content of a course and, therefore, better able to reinforce the program's concepts on the job.

Another way companies have approached management understanding of course content is to have the managers and supervisors of trainees first attend the course themselves. Employers can also create more accountability for supporting training concepts by having the managers and supervisors of trainees serve as instructors for programs.

Follow up. An organization can use many methods to increase the likelihood that the concepts introduced in a training program are applied on the job. Ideally, the following activities should be used to follow up a training program; however, use of any of these methods is likely to improve the transfer of learning from the classroom to the job.

Reinforcement and coaching. Trainees need to be "caught doing something right" and recognized for it. Managers of trainees should be observant of any attempts to apply learning concepts, providing encouragement in the process, rewards when success is achieved and additional assistance if an individual is experiencing difficulty.

At the completion of a training program, participants prepare an action plan that outlines how they'll apply what was learned in the course and measure their success. This is a "learning contract." Learning contracts are most effective when trainees are required to share them with their managers when they return to their jobs, thus creating greater accountability. Even if this is not possible, it can still be effective to have participants share their contracts among themselves and follow up with each other.

DON'T miss this

Post-training meetings. Reassembling a group of training participants who have had the opportunity to apply the concepts introduced in a program can be very beneficial to the learning process. Trainees can discuss and brainstorm ways to overcome barriers they've encountered in attempting to implement new skills, providing mutual help, motivation and support to each other.

✓ ✓ Checklist

Evaluating the training function

Consider asking training participants the following:

☐ To what extent did this program meet the course objectives?
☐ What did you learn from this course?
☐ How will this course impact your job?
☐ How helpful were the following segments (list each segment) to the course?
☐ What recommendations/changes should be made in this program?
☐ What other training would you recommend?
☐ How would you rate the effectiveness of the trainer?

In addition to evaluating each training program, managers must evaluate the entire training effort.

What should be evaluated? Specific parts of the training function that should be reviewed include:

- ◆ **Participants.** Trainee prerequisites must be evaluated to ensure that participants were appropriate and ready.
- ◆ **Trainers.** Instructional staff must be evaluated continuously. Facilities, materials and equipment are never as important as the trainer. Skills, techniques, motivation level and communications are some of the areas involved in evaluating trainers.
- ◆ **Program or course content.** The content itself, sequence in which it is presented and time allocated are important. Duplication, discrepancies and omissions must be identified and addressed. Solicit trainer input along with participants.
- ◆ **Resources.** Input from participants should be solicited on the equipment, facilities and training materials. Include marketing and promotional material. Solicit recommendations to improve each resource.

Training the trainer

Delia, our head of training from the opening scenario, has her training program all worked out. She has designed it to best focus on her company's goal of becoming the leader in long-life light bulb sales in the industry.

The CEO will conduct the first series of sessions, in which she will set forth the company's goals and demonstrate how each job in the company fits into the new product plan.

But since the equipment used to make the long-life bulbs is new and the product is new, Delia is looking for people she can prepare to train others on the use of the machines that make the bulbs. She also needs someone to train the customer service staff about the new product.

How should she go about training the trainers?

Four trainers provided the following model for training trainers (Cathy Petrini, "The Nonprofessional Trainer," *Training and Development Journal,* October 1989, pp. 19–24).

The first steps in developing a training model are:

- ◆ **Purpose.** Establish and write down the purpose of the course.
- ◆ **Objective.** After establishing who and what you're going to instruct, you should set forward learning objectives. The number of learning objectives you establish is based on several factors.
- ◆ **Complexity.** The first of these is the complexity of the subject matter. Complex information may need to be broken down into smaller segments to avoid overwhelming employees with too much material.
- ◆ **Goals.** The second factor to consider in formulating objectives is what goals you are attempting to achieve with the course. Do you want employees to perform an activity independently, start to finish, as a result of the training? Or are you merely providing an overview of the body of knowledge that they will be coached on when they return to their work site?
- ◆ **Time.** The length of time allotted for a course is also a major consideration when developing objectives for a training program. What can be accomplished in two hours of training is very different from a two-day course.

Develop a training guide. The model recommends a training guide as a road map. That way, if you are in front of a classroom and you suddenly freeze in the middle of a sentence, you will have a guide to fall back on.

No one wants to sit passively and be lectured to for hours, so make a trainee contribute to the classroom presentation frequently. According to the model, trainee participation every three minutes is the golden rule. Participation can be in the form of answering questions, reading aloud, critiquing each other's work, role playing and writing on the blackboard.

Trainers should be sensitive to the needs and responses of the trainees. You can measure what individuals are gaining from the material by watching their reactions, asking questions, listening to the meanings of the participants' questions and reading body language.

It is often helpful to begin a training session by asking the employees participating in the program to define their expectations for learning. This process is beneficial for two reasons:

First, it allows the trainer to emphasize or spend additional time on areas of particular interest or concern to the employees attending the program, thus better meeting their needs.

Second, it allows the trainer to immediately identify the expectations that will not be met and to address whether the course is still appropriate for some employees. The trainer may also identify alternative resources employees may use to meet their needs.

Be creative and make the learning experience fun. After developing course objectives, think of as many different ways as possible to achieve those objectives. Use films, slides, exercises, sing-a-longs, costumes, props and games. Formats may also be varied by time. For example, set up a lunch-and-learn approach so that the trainees get lunch and training at the same time.

The trainees should demonstrate in the classroom that they have achieved the learning objectives set for the course. This can be done with exercises or trainee presentations in which the trainees actually take responsibility for teaching and answering questions. The trainees could also go to staff meetings and teach their coworkers, debrief their bosses or friends, or write articles for the company newspaper.

Instructors need to develop a sensitivity to the fact that people learn at different rates and possess different aptitudes. Don't dismiss as "dumb" those who take a little longer to catch on; they could turn out to be fine performers. Approaching the job of training employees with a willingness to help and a friendly attitude will go a long way to offset lack of teaching experience.

"Management development": Train managers too

There is some confusion about what constitutes management development as opposed to training. After all, training teaches management skills, so how is management development different?

The subject matter often overlaps, but usually goes beyond the scope of non-manager training to include supervisory, leadership and strategic elements.

Traditionally, the term "management development" refers to training programs, some of an individual nature, provided to middle- to upper-level managers and executives.

While classroom training certainly is sometimes used in management development programs, the courses are usually more individualized and given to smaller groups. Attendance at specialized seminars, leadership conferences, small groups led by celebrity authors, and multi-summer academic programs are used more often than classroom lecture. Finally, a frequent distinction is that the programs are more personalized to the individual and have more design and content input from the participant.

Executive versus management development. Traditionally, participants of training classes weren't selected from all management levels. Executives and owners didn't participate in the same classes as line employees or supervisors. Middle managers preferred to attend sessions with other managers. Certainly part of this pattern was the desire of the participants.

However, given the trust and sharing that occurs in many training classes, particularly courses concerning management techniques and methods, it was felt that the mixing of management levels could prevent a high degree of candid sharing of information and examples.

Old biases and generalizations disappear slowly. Cost considerations have led many employers to standardize programs to a greater degree and to minimize expensive travel, consultants and other costly delivery methods. However, the distinctions remain to a degree.

Content of management development programs must reflect business needs. Each industry and each company have unique demands that dictate the content of appropriate training and development programs. In most instances, for example, financial expertise is necessary for a manager to be promoted; however, in a few industries, it's not necessary or important.

WHAT you need to know

Further, in most corporations, one or a few individuals may be almost indispensable to the success of the business. Therefore, their deficiencies are offset by adding staff with those abilities and not by demanding that the "star" modify his or her behavior or add new skills. As a result, no fixed listing of skills, abilities and techniques exists for every manager in every business.

The principle for all training, including management development programs, is that the content must be needed by the business. There is no reason for a business to spend shareholders' money on activities that do not have a positive relationship to furthering business goals.

Managing the strategic training function

Management of any function in today's highly competitive and changing business environment is demanding and requires discipline, skill, specialized knowledge and dedication. Managing the training function has, in addition to the demands of management, special challenges including:

◆ **Isolation.** Trainers may not understand the industry and the business as well as line management thinks they should. Trainers typically seek information, education, development experiences and networking from training groups and may not identify with the industry and business. Trainers may not be visible in the workplace outside of the actual training forum. Make sure your trainers understand your business.

◆ **Cost.** It's too often true that training budgets are the first to be reduced, outsourced or eliminated. Training programs, whether purchased or designed in-house, typically are expensive. Delivering myriad training and development programs is staff-intensive, and high overhead work is not highly visible.

◆ **Productivity.** The conventional wisdom is that every training activity should have a direct and positive relationship to improving the bottom line, or the activity shouldn't be done. In the real world, it's sometimes very difficult to quantify the value of programs. In addition, sometimes programs are mandated by executives or regulatory bodies without initial consideration of the costs. Technology is rapidly out-of-date and costly. Too often programs are offered because they're available and not because they're current and needed.

◆ **Change.** Training techniques evolve to use the latest learning theory and research; delivery methods, especially the technology and content of training programs, are constantly changing. Trainees might have the expectation that training must be "on top of" changes in the business and industry (job-specific), educational and psychological developments, and must adapt training programs and content to changing technology at all times.

◆ **Measurement and evaluation.** Traditionally, training programs weren't measured with the same standards, methodology and rigor as line activities. Not only does this cause resentment by line managers and supervisors, it's unfair to investors and owners to spend dollars using unequal standards of value.

◆ **Professionalism.** Trainers are specialized HR staff (whether a part of the human resources function or not) and must accept the demands of confidentiality, objectivity and commitment required of human resources.

◆ **Perception of value.** Too many managers and supervisors do not perceive that trainers add value equal to the cost of the training function.

❓ *The Quiz*

1. Strategic training works best when principles of adult learning are used to design the training program.　❏ True　❏ False

2. Managers have a greater sense of "buy-in" to training when they take the course planned for their employees first.　❏ True　❏ False

3. Training is not one of the methods for introducing new corporate goals or objectives into the workplace.　❏ True　❏ False

4. Which of the following is *not* an advantage of strategic training:
   a. Improved employee performance, including increased quality and quantity of output.
   b. A work force ready to step into jobs created by internal changes.
   c. Promotable employees to fill vacant positions.
   d. Improved employee attitudes and morale leading to reduced absenteeism and turnover and increased customer satisfaction.
   e. Reduction in waste, spoilage and inefficient practices.
   f. Fewer accidents.
   g. None of the above.

Answer key: 1. T; 2. T; 3. F; 4. g.

Strategic retention

Tina has worked as an HR professional in various organizations. In her current job, she's noticed a lack of strategy with respect to turnover and retention. Just this morning at breakfast, she was discussing with two managers how one of their best employees, Theresa, had resigned. Theresa had been with the company for 15 years, but she had found a new job. The managers were laughing about how there are several employees that they wish would resign, but they just won't do it. "They'll stay forever; maybe we should pay them to resign," they joked.

After breakfast, Tina went back to her desk, feeling discouraged, and she had voice mail from Jen, to whom Tina had extended a job offer. Jen said that she was really sorry to turn down the job, but she'd talked to a former employee, and she had "a bad feeling" about the organization. Feeling that things couldn't get any worse that day, Tina was worn out by the time Pradeep stopped by her desk. Pradeep was a newer manager, and he wanted to tell Tina that another employee from his group had quit, and it was time for HR to find him someone else—"someone who will stay a whole year this time," he said, his voice dripping with sarcasm. What can Tina do?

Why retention and turnover matter

In the broadest sense, "employee retention" simply refers to how many of your current employees stick around over a given period of time. Using this definition, a high retention rate would not necessarily be a good thing. For example, it might mean that you're keeping poor performers due to fear of lawsuits, as well as unhappy employees who feel trapped in their jobs due to a poor job market or inertia.

Under that broad definition, retention isn't particularly strategic. In order for your retention practices to be strategic, they must be aligned with the business goals and objectives. This means that you need to know, at a minimum:

◆ Who are the key employees that drive your business strategy?

◆ What motivates those key performers to stay?

◆ What kinds of skills and competencies are needed to make your business successful—today? In the short term? In the long term?

◆ What is the cost of acquiring those skills and competencies through new hires vs. developing them in the existing workforce?

◆ Are there skills, competencies and behaviors that are no longer necessary or desirable in your existing workforce?

◆ What are your plans to transition them and provide the needed skills and behaviors?

When you talk about wanting to maximize retention, you're actually talking about maximizing the number of good employees who stay with you because they want to—because they are invested in the business' success—not because they have to. Sometimes people will leave for reasons beyond your control, but there's a lot you can do to encourage people to stay with your company and be productive.

If you simply hire new people when someone quits, and you take an inactive stance toward poor performers, you'll always be in a reactive position, like Tina's organization. If, however, you want to minimize your turnover costs and retain the employees whose performance you most value, then you must develop a retention strategy that aligns with your business goals.

A retention rate that's too high can be just as bad as one that's too low. You don't want the wrong people staying around.

Costs of turnover. The cost of replacing an employee varies, but there's no question it's expensive—some estimates put the total as high as 200 percent of the employee's annual salary and benefits. This includes a wide variety of expenses, such as advertising, recruiter's salaries and reimbursements for candidates' expenses. You also incur the various start-up costs of hiring someone new, such as administrative expenses and training.

The real cost of preventable turnover is the effect it has on your business. Unmanaged turnover affects your relationships with customers, the morale of employees who stay and institutional memory.

Measuring turnover. According to a 2002 CCH online survey of 520 employers, a surprising number are missing an opportunity to approach retention strategically—a full quarter of respondents report that they don't track turnover rates. Two percent aren't sure if they do or not. This is a big mistake—there's no way to determine if you have a turnover problem if you don't even know how many people are leaving.

Looking at your turnover rates can help you figure out whether your company is doing something to drive people away. As discussed earlier, not all turnover is necessarily bad, and some occurs for reasons that management is neither responsible for nor capable of controlling. Think back to Theresa, who resigned after 15 years. After talking with her, Tina discovers that Theresa recently inherited a great deal of money, so she's planning to devote herself to volunteer work for her favorite charity. Tina realizes that this is not turnover over which the organization has control.

To determine if you truly have a turnover problem—one that negatively impacts both the bottom line and your ability to accomplish business goals—you need to look at your company's "true turnover rate," which excludes employee departures that are unavoidable. Consider the following example:

Your organization has 700 employees on its average payroll. Last year 15 employees were discharged for cause, while 20 employees left voluntarily. Of those 20, four were due to retirement, one was due to a permanent disability and two were the result of family circumstances (one employee left to take care of her elderly parent; another moved when his wife was transferred to a position across the country). Thus, you'd want to subtract out those seven unavoidable departures to get your "true" turnover rate. Here's how you would calculate it:

Net turnover rate 35/700 x 100 = 5%
True turnover rate 28[35-7]/700 x 100 = 4%.

Some industries have higher turnover rates than others. You can obtain turnover data to benchmark your organization against other similar organizations and to determine your turnover rate's strategic significance from the Bureau of Labor Statistics (www.bls.gov/news.release/jolts.toc.htm), industry groups and professional associations.

✔✔✔ Checklist

Interpreting your turnover numbers

Once you know your true turnover rate, the following questions will help you interpret it and determine whether this year's departing employees represent a retention problem that interferes with your company's success.

☐ What is the difference between the turnover rates of men and women?

☐ What is the turnover rate among all demographic groups?

☐ Are there significant differences between any of these groups? If so, why?

☐ How does the true rate compare over time? If the rate has changed, why?

☐ How does the true rate compare to other local employers? Employers within the same industry?

☐ What is the tenure of all employees compared to those who have left?

☐ Were there any "red flags" in the applications of employees who quit or were fired very soon after starting?

☐ Are there any divisions within the company whose turnover is significantly greater than the norm? Why? Is this a deliberate strategy or is it an unintended result?

☐ Are the costs of turnover known, and are they acceptable?

Creating a high–retention culture

Depending on the size of the organization, the industry and the type of employee, turnover averages between 10 and 20 percent annually, with some industries—notably retail, hospitality and health care—trending higher.

Smart organizations make retention a priority, given the significant dollar and time investments inherent in recruiting and training, not to mention the impact high turnover has on customer service, productivity and employee morale, in addition to the bottom line.

DON'T miss this

What do employees want? According to Gregory P. Smith, author of *Here Today, Here Tomorrow: Transforming Your Workforce from High-Turnover to High Retention,* the following attributes are essential to a high retention organization:

◆ **Clearly defined organization direction and purpose.** People want to work for an organization that has purpose and meaning. If you align employees with your mission, you can nurture a more dedicated and productive staff. This fact has enormous implications for strategic HR, for it demonstrates that aligning your "people practices" with a clearly defined and communicated business strategy not only benefits the organization, it also benefits the individual employees and makes your business an employer employees choose.

◆ **Caring management.** It's all about the relationship, yet organizations consistently undervalue soft skills in retention. The quality of an employee's relationship with his or her immediate supervisor is one of the greatest predictors of employee satisfaction and, as a result, retention. Loyalty and respect are values that appear to be reciprocal. Again, this is a place strategic HR can make a difference. Can you measure the costs of unintended turnover in your organization and show their impact on the bottom line? Can you show how changes in supervisory approaches can impact that number? Can you provide cost-effective soft-skills training for managers and supervisors? Of course you can—and in so doing, you can make a difference in the company bottom line.

◆ **Flexibility in scheduling and benefits.** Employees demand flexibility in their jobs because their lives demand it. They'll remain with an employer that guarantees that flexibility.

◆ **Open, straightforward communication.** High-retention workplaces provide a constant communication loop. Don't be afraid to remind employees periodically about the advantages of working for you. Benchmark competitors and communicate advantages. Explore various communication methods, such as focus groups, online databases, hotlines and attitude surveys. Make good communication a priority for all managers, and keep track of your progress in this area. Remember the importance of measurement.

◆ **Energetic and enthusiastic work environment.** Do your
employees enjoy their work? If you can make the work
energizing, employees are more likely to stay.

◆ **Effective performance appraisals.** Effective performance
appraisals help align individual behaviors and performance
with your organization's goals. Stimulating and reinforcing
behaviors that align with the company's meaning and
purpose creates a sense of belonging, along with higher
productivity and more effective employees. Remember
the laughing managers in the opening scenario who were
wishing certain employees would resign? They need
training in doing effective performance appraisals to make
sure that employees who are poor performers are given a
chance to improve, or to ensure that they end up resigning
or being terminated.

◆ **Rewards and recognition.** People need to feel valued and
appreciated. What does your organization do to communicate
effectively that it truly values its employees?

◆ **Training and development.** Workers want the opportunity
to develop their skills. Training and development give people
greater control of their jobs and contribute to increased
loyalty and retention, in addition to the payback in increased
skill development.

◆ **Paying competitive wages.** While decent pay is almost never
sufficient by itself to keep employees around, it is a necessary
baseline step for getting your foot in the retention door.
Raising pay will not automatically lower turnover, but paying
too little—especially during periods of low unemployment—
will contribute to turnover. Strategic HR does its homework
and is able to show senior leadership both the costs of
upgrading compensation structures and the costs—in lost
productivity, in lost opportunity, in turnover—of not staying
competitive in compensation.

◆ **Championing longevity.** Employees appreciate an
employer who honors long service. While signing bonuses
make sense in tight labor markets, smart employers also
recognize and reward employees whose continued service
is valued. Make sure, however, that you are valuing what
makes a difference to your company's success. Simply

rewarding longevity because it's cheap, easy and expected may not do anything to support your company's business strategy or reduce its turnover.

◆ **Respecting employees.** Individualized work sites, supportive relationships with peers and supervisors, and job-specific training are some of the techniques employers can use to strengthen their relationships with employees. And cultivating a culture of respect costs nothing.

◆ **Retention bonuses.** During difficult times—mergers, acquisitions, plant closures, financial difficulties—more and more employers are giving retention bonuses to key employees to encourage continued employment.

Work-life benefits as part of retention program

Work-life benefits form an integral part of employee retention programs. Most retention programs include some type of work-life benefits, such as telecommuting, flex time, more time off and child care.

But what makes sense for your company? Tactical HR looks only at what's new or what's expected in work-life benefits, rather than what programs or policies contribute to the business' strategic success.

Best Practices

M&M® Wednesdays and on-site daycare centers help retain employees at SAS Institute

SAS Institute, a software company in Cary, North Carolina, boasts an enviable retention rate. The turnover rate is only around five percent, according to an interview with Dr. James Goodnight, co-founder, president and CEO of SAS, which was reported by Karla Nagy in "Goodnight Makes All the Right Moves," *Human Capital,* Hughes Communications, Inc.

"[G]enerous benefits and onsite amenities" for employees have helped this software company enjoy 24 years of "double-digit" revenue growth each year. According to Ms. Nagy, SAS

Institute employees enjoy M&M® Wednesdays and an on-site daycare building. The company also maintains roughly a 35-hour workweek in an environment of "flexibility," where face time isn't highly valued, but getting the job done is. In addition, SAS Institute employees also enjoy recreation facilities, free on-site health care and time off to attend their children's soccer games, reports Kim Nash in "SAS Institute: Great for a Reason," Dossiers, *Baseline Magazine, www.baselinemag.com.* SAS is on both the *Fortune* and *Worker Mother's* top 100 places to work lists.

Does this mean that your organization should duplicate SAS Institute's work-life policies? Not necessarily. Instead, look to your own organizational structure, success factors, strategic goals and work force needs. Maybe your organization has a production line that won't accommodate flexible hours during the day, but this doesn't mean you can't provide any flexibility in employees' work lives. Consider instituting creative weekly scheduling that allows production employees a shortened workday once every week or two and doesn't incur overtime or lost-time but allows employees to make that Wednesday night softball practice, for example.

Flexibility as important factor. In technology and professional services companies, if you want to retain employees, it may be especially important to consider work-life benefits that offer flexibility. Increasingly, employees want flexibility in their jobs and will remain with an employer that provides it, according to a Suplee Group survey of former employees at technology and professional services companies. Flexibility in where, when and how work is accomplished, time off for personal matters and other work-life initiatives are valued.

WHAT you need to know

What are the work-life benefits that give employees highly valued flexibility? Take a look at:

◆ Telecommuting;
◆ Flexible work schedules, including summer hours;
◆ Compressed workweeks;
◆ Job sharing;
◆ Time away from work policies that accommodate family and personal events; and
◆ The ability to work at satellite offices.

Make sure your benefit policies enhance employees' abilities to perform their jobs and live their lives.

Worst case scenario

Jackie has an elderly mother who is in poor health. Jackie has to call her mother twice a day, and because her mother is hard of hearing, Jackie has to speak very loudly. Jackie works in a cubicle. Other employees are complaining to Ramiro, the manager, that these "loud and disruptive" phone calls often contain personal information that they would rather not overhear, and they have trouble concentrating on their work while these calls are taking place. Ramiro tells Jackie to stop making these calls. One month later, Jackie, a valuable employee, gives notice. She is going to "find a job that allows her to make sure her mother is all right."

Solution. Because Jackie is a good performer, Ramiro should take steps to keep her from quitting. He should show empathy, and then he should talk to HR to see what work-life benefits are available. For example, she may want to take advantage of a flexible work schedule, or telecommuting, where she can make these calls without disturbing anyone. Or even more simply and cost-effectively, HR could arrange twice-daily access to a private phone and to an elder-care referral service so that Jackie could discuss other care options for her elderly mother.

Gender differences. How many women are in your work force? When asked about factors influencing retention, more women reported that they were interested in flexible work schedules than men, according to the third annual BridgeGate Report, conducted in 2001 by Market Facts TeleNation, Inc. of Chicago for technology search firm BridgeGate LLC, *www.bridgegate.com.*

The difference was not very dramatic, however. Seventeen percent of surveyed female employees were interested in a flexible work schedule versus eleven percent of their male counterparts. If you have many women in your work force, consider whether flexible work schedules may be an especially effective tool in retaining employees.

It's not just work-life benefits that matter to retention. Consider the effect of other benefits on your work force also. Does your benefits package fit with the demographics of your work force? For example, if you have an insignificant number of employees with young children, does offering child care assistance offer a lot of value to your current work force?

Hiring new employees: Retention starts here

Recruiting and hiring are key components of your retention program. Consider the following example:

> *Etta, the recruiter for ABC Incorporated, has recently made several hires. However, Etta has noticed that many of them don't seem to be thriving at ABC. One even left after lunch on the first day and never came back. Does the way ABC makes its hiring decisions affect the number and quality of the employees retained? Not considering her hiring policies in a vacuum, Etta wonders how she can better tailor her practices to best compliment both the organization's retention goals and its business objectives.*

Etta's thinking is on the right track—retention planning does start much earlier than one might think. Remember, the candidates you're most interest in attracting to your organization are the ones with the skills and qualifications that will make them desirable elsewhere. A thoughtful, careful interview process allows you to spot the "good ones" but it's also an opportunity for you to sell the candidates on your organization.

If you get people off on the right foot from the very beginning, which includes the interview process, they're much more likely to view your organization as a place to settle in for the long haul and develop a career. On the other hand, if they're turned off during the interview, you won't even get them in the door in the first place.

When it goes wrong—remedying bad hires

Sometimes, despite your best efforts, a few "bad apples" will inevitably worm their way into your organization at some point. When this happens, don't be afraid to cut them loose.

Mis-hires can affect your retention rates negatively because they tend to drive good people away. They also hurt your bottom line because they occupy positions that could be filled more successfully by others.

Surveys show that most managers know within the first year whether they've made a hiring mistake, according to a piece in the November 2001 issue of *Employee Recruitment & Retention* (adapted from "Hire without fear," by Michael Barrier, in *Nation's Business*). However, most wait at least a year to fix it. "While turnover is costly, failing to act on a bad hire may cause even more regret in the long run—particularly if the person disrupts workplace camaraderie or alienates customers."

Southwest Airlines, which has some of the highest retention rates around, knows the value of acting promptly to remedy bad hires. In *Nuts! Southwest Airlines' Crazy Recipe for Business and Personal Success,* Kevin and Jackie Frieberg note one of Southwest's cardinal rules: "Be religious about hiring the right people. If you make the wrong hiring decision, within the first 90 days make the tough decision to say good-bye."

Worst case scenario

Fredricka hired the "employee from hell" for an engineering sales position. Jerry had a master's degree in engineering from a reputable school and 10 years relevant experience from a foreign-owned company. However, he was so inept that the organization had to move him to inside sales. He was no good at that either.

What happened? Turns out that Jerry's former employer never adequately supervised his work. When the company went out of business in the United States, it wasn't careful about the references it handed out. Also, an industrial psychologist who interviewed and tested Jerry strongly recommended against his hiring. But Fredricka thought he was too good to pass up, given his education, experience and charming interview manner.

Now Fredricka is faced with dismissing Jerry, and Jerry has hired a lawyer to sue for wrongful discharge.

Solution: Fredricka needs to make sure that all employees are hired with the understanding that their employment is provisional for the first three months—meaning they can be fired at any time if it's not working out. If Jerry's signed such an agreement, Fredricka will probably be able to terminate him without legal penalty.

In most states, "at will" employment laws generally allow employers to fire employees for any nondiscriminatory reason or no reason. However, having a probationary policy in place puts poor performers on heightened notice that they're not guaranteed a spot with you forever. Make sure you're clear that continued employment is not guaranteed, even after the end of the probationary period.

Those activities are just basic compliance. To behave strategically, HR will need to reevaluate its overall recruiting and selection practices, looking at not just turnover rates and cost per hire, but also effectiveness per hire—in other

words, how many hires turn out like Jerry, looking good on paper and at the interview but performing poorly?

Once HR has examined what's working and what isn't, by documenting and tracking those metrics, it can recommend changes in the process to ensure that only high-quality candidates are eligible for hire. In this instance, for example, how did Fredricka override the recommendation of the industrial psychologist? Should that policy be revisited? Do hiring managers need more training or just more coaching? Or was this an unavoidable "accident" that revisited policies couldn't address?

Orientation programs

Once you've made the hire, it's critical that your organization make a good first impression. Orientation is the **formal** process of introducing new employees to the organization, their supervisors, coworkers and jobs. Remember, there will always be an "informal process" that may support or may conflict with the formal process. While the new hire orientation can start to seem "routine" to the HR professional and anything but strategic, it's very important to the new employee, and ultimately, your retention efforts.

Although you can't exercise direct control over the "unofficial" orientation programs that take place in the workplace, you can ensure that the formal orientation process is consistent with the values and cultures of your organization. If the formal process is dramatically different than the reality in the workplace, the formal program is likely to be discounted by the new employee and will prove to be ineffective.

DON'T miss this

Employees' impressions of their organization aren't just a "people" matter. Dissatisfaction may translate into turnover, which translates into dollars spent.

Former employees as part of retention program

If turnover and retention happen without any analysis in your company, like they seemed to do in Tina's organization, you're ignoring sound business reasons in support of conducting exit interviews and maintaining relationships with your former employees. Do the following examples sound familiar?

> *McRae decided to be a stay-at-home mom after her baby's first birthday. She told her manager that she would have loved to move to part-time work instead, but her manager just assumed the company "doesn't do that" and he didn't consult with HR, so HR never knew about McRae's interest in part-time work.*
>
> *Thomas went to work for a competitor after more than two decades with your organization. Everyone was shocked at the news, but no one directly asked him why.*
>
> *Kimberly quit "suddenly" according to her manager, but you know that Kimberly had voiced complaints about the manager several times to coworkers and her manager's boss, without any action ever taken.*
>
> *Michael, a long-time, well-thought-of employee, hasn't resigned. But he did transfer to a different business unit. Because he stayed with the company, his manager didn't consider that Michael's reasons for leaving the group might apply to coworkers—and they might leave the organization entirely.*

Exit interviews

Exit interviews are an enormously important part of any retention strategy and provide valuable information for formulating the business strategy as well. If you know why people leave, you'll be in much better shape to fix problems before they drive people away. Also, for employees like McRae, who are leaving for personal reasons, a frank discussion may enable you to come up with a compromise rather than lose them completely.

Even if they're really set on leaving your organization, employees appreciate being treated with respect on their way out and having an opportunity to be heard. Some of them may also want to work for you again someday, and this is much more likely if the departure is on good terms.

WHAT you need to know

When people return to your organization from other jobs, they invariably bring a new set of skills and experiences that may make them even better employees than when they left. For example, they will be able to look at your organization with an outsider's eye, while at the same time understanding your history and realities.

When preparing your plan for exit interviews, be sure to select carefully who will conduct it. The interviewer must be someone with genuine interest and concern for the employee's circumstances. Often this will be someone from HR. Don't forget about employees who are transferring within your organization, like Michael in the previous example. Frequently, they will be transferring for a better opportunity, but sometimes they will have valuable information about where they're leaving.

DON'T miss this

Don't waste this opportunity. There's a wealth of information regarding retention available from the exit interview, but if the interviewer approaches this as a mundane task, that opportunity is wasted.

Do your homework to get the most valuable retention information out of the exit interview. Make an appointment in advance to allow both the interviewer and interviewee to prepare. Don't schedule it for the employee's last day, as that day tends to be "lost." The interviewer should be familiar with the employee's performance record and should have spoken with the employee's supervisor. Conduct the interview in a private setting where the employee can speak freely.

✓ ✓ **Checklist**

*Information you need
from departing employees*

Answers to the following questions will give you insight into why someone is leaving:

☐ Why are you leaving?
☐ If you're going to another job, what does that job offer that your current job does not?
☐ What factors contributed to your accepting a job here? Were your expectations realized?
☐ How would you evaluate your salary in comparison to the work you performed?
☐ What did you enjoy about working here?
☐ What did you dislike about working here (even things that didn't contribute to your leaving)?
☐ What comments or suggestions do you have for making this a better place to work?
☐ Would you recommend our organization to a friend or relative as a good place to work? Why or why not?

Make note of any particular job, manager or department that seems to have higher than expected turnover. Think back to Pradeep, the manager whose employees kept leaving within their first year. Maybe the problem isn't HR's recruitment and hiring; maybe the problem is Pradeep. If you don't track problem areas, you won't have a big-picture view of what's really happening.

Exit interviews can't help you with your retention strategy if the results are tossed in a file or read once and thrown away. You need regular active review of this information to spot trends, and to develop a business case for retention efforts that serve the business strategy.

DON'T
miss
this

Alumni relationships

Alumni: They're not just for schools anymore. Former employees—a.k.a. alumni—are a good resource for a variety of reasons. For example, they can continue to help you directly with projects, as contractors or in other nontraditional work arrangements. They may also be willing to throw business your way if you do the same for them. Finally, alumni are a rich source of valuable contacts.

WHAT you need to know

> While alumni can be your biggest champions, they can also be your worst enemies, spreading horror stories about your organization. You aren't likely to have a productive future relationship with every former employee, but do your best to remedy any active ill will. Tina, in the opening scenario, has encountered this problem with Jen, who's heard bad things about the organization. Tina needs to consider how the organization can foster productive alumni relationships in order to avoid this in the future.

Re-hiring alumni. When should you re-hire an employee who voluntarily left to work somewhere else, or who left the job market for awhile? While the loyalty that is demonstrated by many consecutive years of employment should be rewarded, people who choose to leave for one reason or another should not be looked on unfavorably.

An employee who leaves might find that the very act of leaving has made your company look better to them. Maybe he thought the grass was greener somewhere else, and he finds that it's not. The employee in that situation will want to return, this time to stay. And an employee who has been trained and then returns may constitute a relatively low-cost hire.

You may also want to recruit former employees actively. But consider whether or not your corporate culture is hospitable to returning employees. If your culture sends a covert, or direct, message that former employees aren't welcome, you'll have to change the culture by persuading employees that former employees tend to have more experience and perspective. That is, it makes good business sense to hire this experience and perspective at no cost to your organization.

Are you concerned about rewarding employees who leave? If your program is targeted exclusively at former high performers, you are hiring proven talent with an expanded skill set. You are effectively outsourcing some of your training and development costs.

DON'T miss this

⁇ *The Quiz*

1. Which of the following attributes is not typical of high retention organizations?
   a. Clearly defined organization, direction and purpose.
   b. Open communication.
   c. Training and development.
   d. Managers who lack the respect of their organizations.

2. If an employee is a poor hire, it's usually not evident for at least a year. ❑ True ❑ False

3. Costs of replacing an employee may include which of the following?
   a. Advertising for open position.
   b. Reimbursement for candidate's expenses.
   c. Training the new hire.
   d. All of the above.

4. Work-life programs and retention policies are unrelated. ❑ True ❑ False

Answer key: 1. d; 2. F; 3. d; 4. F.

Measuring success

> *Yared was thrilled to see a sharp reduction in turnover this year, following two rather tumultuous years of transition. HR's change management initiatives have really paid off! And, since he had carefully tracked turnover costs, Yared was able to go to his CEO with solid evidence of the strategic benefit of their efforts. The executive was pleased to see the numbers, but urgently wanted to know, "Do these turnover figures tell us* who *is leaving? Are we holding on to our key performers, or just encouraging the dead weight to hang around?" Yared was embarrassed to admit he didn't have the answer.*
>
>   *What more strategic data could he have collected?*

What are metrics?

There's an old adage that says, "What gets measured gets managed." It's a line that's often repeated in business, because it rings true. When you measure something, you come to understand it, to gain control. You also come to see and recognize its worth.

The Saratoga Institute, a human capital management firm known for its benchmarking tools, is driven by the theory that "If results aren't measured, you can't understand them. If you can't understand them, you can't control them. If you can't control them, you can't improve them. Then, by definition, you can't manage them."

As you strive to align HR initiatives to your organization's business goals and step outside the familiar transactional role, you'll need a clear picture of the work force you manage and the effective HR operations by which you manage it. Plus, to track your progress as a strategic player, you'll need tools to evaluate whether you're on the right track. After all, if you don't have some way of quantifying your HR and business objectives, how will you know when you've achieved them? To these ends, the use of HR metrics is vital. In fact, one HR metrics conference called human capital measurement the "Holy Grail" of HR executives!

WHAT you need to know

Metrics are numbers that indicate how well an organization is performing in a specific area. They provide the context around which that performance should be analyzed. Metrics are often expressed as a percentage (for example, percentage return on investment), or sums (for example, total quarterly revenue).

("A Seat at the Table: How Smart HR Departments Win With BI." Cognos Incorporated, November 2002.)

What metrics do HR departments use?

A study by Mercer Human Resource Consulting surveyed HR leaders at some 300 organizations and asked which standard HR or human capital metrics they were using. "There are literally hundreds of metrics used by human resource professionals today, ranging from the most basic to highly complex scorecards and work force analytics," said David Knapp, a senior consultant in Mercer's technology and operations practice and the study's author. "What we found is that most organizations tend to track and report a few basic measures. However, leading employers are attempting to measure in areas such as employee skill levels, promotions or training program effectiveness, and link these measures to business results."

Here's what survey respondents said they measured:

Use of HR Metrics	
HR Metrics	**Percent of Employers Using Metrics**
Employee attitudes	78%
Turnover	57%
Satisfaction with HR service	56%
Outsourcing costs	52%
Service center operations	49%
HR transactions processed	43%
Staffing process/outcomes	41%
Training utilization	40%
HR consulting services utilization	39%
Training program effectiveness	38%
Promotions	32%
Employee skill levels	24%
Mercer Human Resource Consulting, "Transforming HR for Business Results."	

Why should you measure?

When you measure the success of your efforts, you demonstrate that you take those efforts seriously. As Staffing.org notes, "By not accurately measuring their performance, staffing and other human resources operations make a statement to the rest of the organization that their work is not valuable."

Yet initially, metrics wasn't an easy sell to HR departments and executives. "Why the reluctance? For many, the idea of quantifying what's in the hearts and minds of people runs counter to their basic values. Intuitively, they feel measuring people as if they were widgets is distasteful," notes Robert J. Grossman, an attorney and professor of management studies at Marist College. ("Measuring Up: Measuring human resources performance," *HR Magazine*, January, 2000).

So what are the advantages of measurement?

Measuring creates accountability. It allows you to show the concrete value of the HR department's work. While you may have been successful at sending the general message that HR operations add crucial value, with metrics you can demonstrate your worth in a tangible way.

Measuring provides opportunity. Metrics allow you to observe in stark relief any operational problems that may be undermining your organization's success. While an ongoing issue might be silently nagging at you, once you see the concrete negative effects, you'll be spurred into action.

Measuring breeds success. With the ability to identify and fix what's broken, demonstrate value to key leaders, and align your efforts to business strategy, metrics can help you become an invaluable member of your organization's leadership.

A+ *Best Practices*

Top companies measure HR functions

Consulting group Best Practices LLC, after performing an intensive benchmarking study of the business practices of 10 top U.S. companies, identified characteristics that Coca-Cola Corp., Entergy Inc., Mirant Inc. and others have in common. Key among them? The top employers measure specific HR functions on a continuing basis to determine return on investment (ROI) and contributions to the bottom line. The benchmarked companies use HR scorecards to identify, track and report important HR measurements and link incentive and merit compensation for their HR staff to the performance or scorecard results.

Best Practices LLC, www.best-in-class.com

Is your organization ready?

What about your organization? Is it time for your department to adopt HR metrics?

"Metrics only flourish when they are planted in the rich soil of a measurement culture," notes HR consultant Peter Weddle. "That means you have at least one champion above you who believes passionately in the importance of metrics and will give you political cover ... And it means that the organization is willing to put money on the table. You have to gauge the reality of the organization and where your function is in the enterprise. If it's more talk than walk—it's probably not a good time to implement metrics. Instead, try to find ways to nurture that soil, that acceptance of the importance of human capital, first.

"The irony is that people think metrics can lead to that understanding, and it's really the other way around. You have to have the fundamental belief in the importance of human capital before you can invest in metrics successfully." (Source: Interview with Peter Weddle, "Courage Under Hire," Workforce.com).

There's no room for pessimism, though. A survey of HR executives conducted by Cognos, Incorporated revealed that 84 percent of respondents believed their organization's investment in HR measurement will increase over the next five years. Will you be ready?

✓ ✓ **Checklist**

Is HR ready for additional measurement and evaluation?

Review the statements below. Do they apply to your organization? Answer "agree" or "disagree" to each.

☐ Our organization is undergoing significant change.
☐ There is pressure from senior management to measure results of HR solutions.
☐ Our organization has a culture of measurement and has established a variety of measures, including some for HR.
☐ The HR function currently has a very low investment in measurement and evaluation.

Continued on next page

Continued from previoust page

- [ ] Our organization has experienced more than one HR disaster in the past.
- [ ] The HR team would like to be the leaders in accountability.
- [ ] The image of the HR function is less than satisfactory.
- [ ] Our clients are demanding that HR solutions show bottom-line results.
- [ ] The HR function competes with other functions for resources.
- [ ] There is increased emphasis on linking HR solutions to the strategic direction of the organization.

"Measuring HR's Return on Investment," presented by Jack Phillips, Ph.D., Jack Phillips Center for Research, a Division of Franklin Covey, at the 55th Annual Conference and Exposition of the Society for Human Resource Management, Orlando, Florida, June 2003.

WHAT you need to know

How many of these statements rang true? If you agreed with 7–10, your organization is primed to implement HR metrics, and the executive team will welcome your efforts. Agreed with 4–6? You might be a bit ahead of the curve, but start now to adopt some measures that won't require large resource outlays. If only 1–3 applied to your organization's current environment, the demand for metrics won't exist. Then what? You can begin to test the waters with some internal functional measurements within your HR department, and wait for the organization to catch up.

How should you measure?

When it comes to the effective use of metrics, context is everything. A measurement taken in a vacuum, without a purpose or connection to a tangible problem or objective, has little business value. According to Marcia Barkley, an independent consultant and 15-year HR professional, "Measuring isn't very useful until you start *making comparisons.*" The data becomes valuable when you see it run its course over time, and analyze how it correlates with other measures, including non-HR data.

Consider the data or transactions you record and track. Why do you track them? Is it "because we've always kept track"? Is it because your boss is curious? Or because the data reveal important clues that help you further concrete goals? More important, do your metrics isolate the other potential variables that contribute to a business problem? Do your numbers reflect *causation,* or just *correlation?*

"For a metric to be truly valuable, it must be an indicator of some characteristic that can be directly related to cause and effect," notes consultant John Sullivan, a thought leader in HR metrics. For example, "A low offer-to-acceptance ratio may be an indicator of recruiter performance or compensation, but it also may indicate a poor interview process, low firm desirability and even instability in the employment market."

What makes a metric?

According to John Sullivan, "For your metrics to have value to yourself and others, they must:

◆ *Relate directly to the company's strategic business objectives.*

◆ *Tell a clear, concise story that won't be easily dismissed."*

Dr. John Sullivan, head and professor of the Human Resource Management College of Business at San Francisco State University, April 21, 2003, as reported in Workforce.com question/answer board.

What is your purpose for collecting the data? Looking again at the offer-to-acceptance ratio metric, consider whether the measurement captures the information you really need. If your HR objective is to increase your acceptance rate, the metric you've implemented can tell you whether your acceptance rate is problematic. But it can't tell you *why*—or how to improve upon it. You'll need to dig deeper for that.

Metrics are used to focus our efforts. To be effective and reliable, then, the metrics you implement must be *actionable.* And they must include specific definitions, performance targets, thresholds, data sources and indicators of historical performance. ("A Seat at the Table: How Smart HR Departments Win With BI." Cognos Incorporated, November 2002.)

WHAT you need to know

Know your business metrics

To be a strategic partner, you need to do more than implement HR metrics. You'll also need to become familiar with the business metrics used by your executive team and other functional areas within the company and industry. Learn to assess what the standard business measures indicate and how to spot potential trouble.

In-depth expertise isn't necessary, but an understanding of *why* these measures matter, and how HR functions impact them, will be a critical strategic asset.

Here are some standard business metrics that merit further study:

◆ Money (revenue or expense);
◆ Time (to respond, process or deliver);
◆ Quantity (volume or frequency);
◆ Quality (errors or defects); and
◆ Human reaction (employee or customer attitudes).

You already know what you do each day profoundly affects each of these variables. What will make your efforts even more valuable is the ability to show measured, tangible evidence of that impact.

What should you measure?

What you measure depends in no small part on your organization's strategic direction. Certainly your HR operations have core functions you'll want to measure in order to better align the department with the larger mission. But the specific business goals must also inform what you measure, and what measures will indicate success.

That means there is no cookie-cutter solution, since so much will be dictated by your particular organization and its strategic goals. "Metrics that are most useful need to be specially designed for each organization," advises Professor Robert J. Grossman. What's important for a manufacturing company to measure will be very different than the metrics a financial services company might adopt.

And the variance isn't just across industries. An insurance company looking to grow by expanding its customer base will have different business drivers than a competitor whose growth strategy is to sell additional insurance products to existing customers. What different human capital needs might there be? How can you measure how well HR meets those needs?

Here's how to select the best metrics for your organization:

Ask your colleagues

Consult with your organization's key leaders to ensure the metrics you've adopted will best capture the strategic information most essential to your organization. Ask, what metrics matter most to them? The answer must factor into the metrics you adopt. According to Evans and Lermusiaux, working in tandem with professionals outside HR has the following benefits:

- ◆ Feedback from your peers will help to increase the value of your data.
- ◆ You have access to credible resources that can poke holes in your methodology, if faulty.
- ◆ Partnership generates buy-in. If key players are part of the process, then they must support the resulting data.
- ◆ The benefit of your peers' credibility is extended to you, and further helps create acceptance.
- ◆ These advantages in turn validate your data; validated data is more value-added and strategic.

"How to Make HR Technology Speak: Extract Meaningful Data to Manage Your Business." Presented by Kristie Evans, HRLogistics and Yves Lermusiaux, iLogos Research, at 55th Annual Conference & Exposition of the Society for Human Resource Management, Orlando, Florida, June 2003.

Note too that, with the growing recognition of the value of human capital, and as the HR function gains in strategic importance, your executive team may *want* to give direct input into how the organization's human assets and HR operations are evaluated. In a 2003 survey of corporate chief financial officers, respondents expressed a strong interest in collaborating with HR to measure the company's human capital asset. ("Human capital management: the CFO's perspective," Mercer Human Resource Consulting.)

DON'T miss this

Don't forget about your line managers! Strategic HR leaders say it's important to track metrics that line managers value. Meaningful measures must also be meaningful to your customers; in the case of the HR department, that primarily means your line organizations. What data do your line managers and department heads need in order to drive business goals and serve their own strategic roles? Providing the information they need will add further value to your measurement efforts.

Consider the standard HR metrics

The Saratoga Institute has identified many of the standard tools for measuring HR department effectiveness as well as human capital performance. These traditional metrics fall under the broad categories of organizational effectiveness; compensation; benefits; separations; and staffing:

Sample HR metrics

Organizational effectiveness

Revenue factor: revenue divided by FTEs (full-time equivalents)

Expense factor: total expense / FTEs

Income factor: revenue 1 expense / FTEs

Human investment ratio:
    revenue 1 (total expense 1 comp & ben) / comp & ben

HR expense percent: HR expense / total expense

HR headcount ratio: total organization FTEs / total HR FTEs

HR investment factor: HR expense / total FTEs

HR separation rate: HR separations / HR headcount

Compensation

Compensation revenue factor: compensation costs / revenue

Compensation expense factor: compensation costs / expense

Supervisory comp percent:
    supervisory comp costs / comp costs

Benefits

Benefit revenue factor: benefits cost / revenue

Benefit expense factor: benefits cost / total expense

Benefit compensation factor: benefits cost / compensation

Healthcare factor: health program costs / covered employees

Separations (Calculate for total, exempt and nonexempt)

Separation rate: total separations / total headcount

Voluntary separation rate: voluntary separations / headcount

Involuntary separation rate: involuntary separations / headcount

Staffing (Calculate for total, exempt and nonexempt; can be separated into internal and external categories)

Accession rate: total hires / total headcount

Add rate: total add hires / total headcount

Replacement rate: total replacement hires / total headcount

Cost per hire: total hiring costs / total hires

Time to fill: total days to fill a requisition / acceptances

Time to start: total days to start / requisitions filled

In addition to these metrics, a limitless array of measurements—some proven, others more innovative—related to HR functions can be applied to strategic benefit. Indeed, the list above merely skims the surface of possible assessment tools. Consider just a few of the metrics John Sullivan suggests you analyze:

◆ Revenue per employee;

◆ Speed of promotions of hires;

◆ Number or percentage of hires taken from direct competitors;

◆ Number or percentage of EEO complaints or lawsuits;

◆ Cost of vacant positions;

◆ "Headcount fat," or excess employees; and

◆ Behavioral or performance changes following training.

In short, you don't need to rely on the standard HR metrics—or even the newest measurement tools the experts suggest—to implement metrics that have value and work best for your particular organization. In fact, using the standard metric set while your organization cries for alternative evaluation methods can undermine your strategic aims.

WHAT you need to know

HR metrics should not simply count successful transactions! As HR departments shift their focus from a transactional perspective to a strategic one, the measurements they implement must support this effort. Use clear-cut indicators of success and failure, as determined by how they further strategic business goals.

Traditional metrics revisited

As noted above, before implementing the tried-and-true HR metrics, consider whether they are the proper tools for your organization's strategic goals. Keep in mind that many of these measures were formulated before the real advent of "strategic human resources." And note further that top HR thought leaders are taking a second, more critical look at the traditional stand-bys. So should you. Consider these examples:

Cost-per-hire. One of the most commonly used staffing metrics is the cost-per-hire, long calculated as a standard measure of recruiting costs. Yet the traditional cost-per-hire metric has come under fire of late, derided as having little meaningful value to business goals. As Staffing.org asks, what does cost-per-hire mean? "What does it mean to say our organization's Cost-per-Hire is $4,000? What do you do with this information? What do you learn from this figure? Is this good, bad, or indifferent? Should you aim for $3,500 per hire next year? If so, why?" ("Staffing Metrics Mini-Toolkit," Staffing.org.)

This figure gives some information about how efficiently your recruiting team is carrying out its work. But it doesn't tell you whether these efforts are generating the strategic payoff. How have your expert recruiting skills landed *quality* employees who will further the organization's mission and goals? Cost-per-hire metrics won't reflect this information.

That's why many HR consultants now advise replacing the cost-per-hire metric with a better measure: **quality-of-hire**. Assessing the quality of employees you've brought in through your recruiting efforts has far greater strategic value. After all, as John Sullivan stresses, "hiring cheap is easy. But quality is often expensive. And quality hires have a better return on investment." A quality-of-hire metric thus can prevent you from crafting a cost-per-hire driven solution that is penny-wise and pound-foolish.

Turnover costs. Let's look back at Yared's turnover costs metric, for example. You can track your organization's turnover rates, identify cost-per-turnover, and provide some indicators of the financial impact of employee turnover. What, then, are you to do with this data? If you fixate on reducing these costs, which the traditional metric might suggest, you'll look at this number and decide you need to reduce turnover across the board.

But this is where you take a step back and survey the larger picture. You know that a certain amount of turnover is healthy and beneficial; you don't want to keep poor performers forever. If you reduce turnover to cut this expense, what will that do to your revenue-per-employee numbers?

You need a more sophisticated analysis than that. You require more detailed numbers. What to do? Opt for more meaningful metrics: Track retention rates in aggregate with employee performance metrics and uncover turnover data broken down by higher performers, average performers and low performers. If you could identify high turnover rates among low performers—so what? But if your top performers are leaving en masse? That would demand strategic action.

While traditional HR metrics are an invaluable source of data and strategic information, be prepared to alter them, and add more, as the unique needs of your organization require.

Look beyond your organization

Like other strategic leaders within your organization, you need to look beyond its walls. It's vital for you to keep a constant eye on key competitors, industry trends and the business climate. Another benefit of an outside perspective is the opportunity to use benchmarks, to gauge your practices and measure your successes against other employers. Are your recruiting costs in line with your industry? Can your organization claim a higher revenue-per-employee than your strongest competitor? Gathering this data puts your HR department's successes in sharp focus—or offers a stark picture of where further strategic effort is needed.

Remember that turnover costs metric discussed previously? Standing alone, the figure indicates very little. But *comparing* the data can tell you a lot. If your numbers show your turnover rate is 10 percent higher than your industry's standard, then you have a problem!

You can obtain reliable benchmark data from a number of sources:

◆ Network with other companies within your industry and form a group for the purpose of sharing information.

◆ Consult The Saratoga Institute, Staffing.org, SHRM, and other organizations that create standardized metrics. (It's useful to borrow and implement some standard metrics for comparative purposes. But remember: To maximize the strategic value, you'll still need to customize your own "suite" of measurement tools for your organization's unique needs.)

◆ Consult industry or trade organizations. Many professional associations collect such data from their members and produce benchmark reports.

DON'T miss this

Numerous resources offer free information on staffing-related metrics. These sources are useful starting points from which to develop and customize your organization's metrics.

Getting the numbers right

The metrics game is new to many HR professionals. And, more comfortable with people than with the cold hard world of numbers (if we are to believe the common stereotypes, that is!), HR professionals have made some missteps along the way. Here are a few common metrics mistakes that Evans and Lermusiaux have identified:

◆ Too many metrics.

◆ Metrics for the sake of metrics.

◆ Metrics not driving the intended action.

◆ Lack of follow-up.

"How to Make HR Technology Speak: Extract Meaningful Data to Manage Your Business." Presented by Kristie Evans, HRLogistics and Yves Lermusiaux, iLogos Research, at 55th Annual Conference & Exposition of the Society for Human Resource Management, Orlando, Florida, June 2003.

These errors reflect either the failure to gather appropriate data (in this case, information overload); or a failure to turn the information into concrete action. Have you already committed one of these blunders? You're not alone: A 2001 survey by the Corporate Leadership Council (an HR research organization) revealed that most HR managers lacked confidence that their HR metrics were aligned with corporate strategy. ("A Seat at the Table: How Smart HR Departments Win With BI," Cognos Incorporated.)

It certainly is easy to see how such mistakes are possible! Perhaps they are inevitable outgrowths of our enthusiasm to demonstrate strategic value and add still further value. "We have made significant strides in measuring how human resource initiatives help the bottom line," notes performance consultant Jerry Donini. "However, as HR professionals eagerly communicate the results of new studies to business leaders, they must look past some of the smoke and mirrors and carefully examine the underlying assumptions and facts."

With respect to the information-gathering obstacles, success depends, as noted throughout this chapter, on carefully aligning your metrics to the strategic objectives. Taking the time to assess those goals can avoid unnecessary measurement for measurement's sake.

Donini offers some additional data-collection "red flags" to watch out for:

- ◆ **Spurious correlations.** "The data looks convincing and the correlations are statistically significant, but after closer inspection it just doesn't make sense." Donini offered as an example a study showing a link between specific HR practices and shareholder value. While there was a real correlation, it wasn't clear that there was an actual cause-and-effect relationship between them.

- ◆ **Semantics.** Avoid using terms like "shareholder value" interchangeably with "business results," "financial performance," "economic results" and "business success." Such mixed usage can mislead and misinform, Donini notes. For example, in the boom market of the late 1990s, "shareholder value" had little relationship to actual bottom-line performance. Careful usage can prevent you from undermining the credibility of your numbers.

- ◆ **Short time horizons.** Studies must be conducted and measurements evaluated over a long period to determine a real relationship between HR's strategic initiatives and your organization's business outcomes, Donini says.

Jerry Donini, "Studying HR's Worth: Tips for evaluating the research," HR.com.

WHAT you need to know

If at first you don't succeed ...

Don't fret too much if your metrics aren't flawless the first time out; fine tuning will be inevitable. "It is critical that the people involved in these efforts understand that bringing something under a measurement regime involves a commitment to constant renewal and the search for ever better tools." (John Sumser, Electronic Recruiting.) And your organization's leadership will tolerate some trial and error in getting the numbers just right. It's a sign of continual improvement and demonstrates your ongoing commitment to furthering business goals.

It's not the data, it's what you do with it!

"What is important about measurement is not the measure itself but the attention paid to the problem as the result of measuring it." (John Sumser, Electronic Recruiting.) The corollary holds true also: If you fail to give attention to the problems or opportunities you've identified through the use of metrics, then those metrics are of little worth. As HR consultant Weddle notes as well, "It's not about doing numbers. It's about figuring out what numbers mean and using that knowledge to do things better."

Take action!

You've determined the most important metrics to implement for the unique needs of your organization. You've collected the data, crunched the numbers. Now what? Time now to apply the information to strategic problem solving. Here's where the metrics pay off; it's where your professional knowledge and skills really add strategic value.

✓ **Checklist**
✓
  Metrics-based action steps
  ☐ Communicate what you've found to your
     organization's key leaders.
☐ Based on your findings, identify improvement goals.
☐ Chart a plan of attack, using measurable objectives.
☐ Implement the changes you have identified.
☐ Measure and monitor the progress of your strategic goals.
☐ Communicate the changes you've implemented and the
   progress achieved.
☐ Review, reassess and revise your metrics as needed, or as
   business goals change.

Metrics in context

Now a stern caveat about metrics is in order: "The downside of metrics is that it can lead to financial measures myopia," warns William Brown, professor of management at Marist College. "You may become so fixated on trying to measure financial aspects of human management that you forget to deal with the people aspects of the business. If you become too focused on the financial measures, you may drive out creativity and innovation. You want to maintain a balanced perspective—think of what it is you're trying to do. Will an overemphasis on financial measures change the organization's culture so as to have a negative effect?"

This is a valid concern—one you're well qualified to handle. You know, perhaps even more intuitively than your CFO or even CEO, that quantitative data can be a great asset in making strategic business decisions, but there are limits to the usefulness of even the most powerful decision support tools. Ultimately, there's no substitute for sound judgment and a keen understanding of people.

Highlights

Work force analytics: measurement and beyond ...

Metrics are invaluable for gauging how well you've aligned your efforts with the larger goals of your organization. Work force analytics can help you do even more. Work force analytics are software-based business intelligence systems that allow sophisticated analysis, not just of transactional HR data, but also enterprise-wide information, such as customer and supplier records or financial data. Analytics enable you to "aggregate" this wide range of data and analyze the *interplay* between the information.

DON'T miss this

With work force analytics, it's not just about measuring; it's about taking those numbers and really crunching them for a sophisticated analysis of your employee population and its operational role. The ability to apply work force analytics can add even greater value to your strategic role.

Consultant Marcia Barkley provided some examples of the utility of analytics to HR, in the area of compensation. "They can help a company model how different changes in incentive and benefits could affect productivity among different employee segments. Another question [analytics] can help answer is, Do the employees in the top quartile of the salary range produce proportionally more than those paid in the middle or bottom of the range?" ("Putting Analytics to Work," Samuel Greengard, *Workforce Management.*)

But analytics add strategic value outside the narrow HR realm as well. Here's a closer look at how work force analytics can help address an organization's operational challenges on a broader scale:

Best Practices

Using work force analytics

With more than 2,000 employees scattered throughout 69 locations worldwide, the International Finance Corporation (a World Bank subsidiary and provider of loan and equity financing for private sector projects in the developing world), faced considerable challenges in building an efficient high-performance organization.

Joe Fucello, IFC's human resources program officer, described the problems its HR department faced: "Beyond the PeopleSoft transactional system, the HR department was largely paper-based. It lacked a strong data foundation as well as the means to analyze data for informed decision-making. There were few people in the HR department skilled in data analysis and the only tool available was a home-grown data extraction tool to download raw data from our transaction system into a spreadsheet. The seemingly simple inquiries were becoming more and more difficult to answer; if two people were asked the same question, they'd likely provided two different answers.... To be a credible corporate partner, we knew we needed a more integrated view of our operations, supported by sound and accurate data analysis."

Fucello's team took these steps:

◆ **They evaluated the quality of their data and cleaned it up.** "Although painful [this step] has proved critical in improving the accuracy and reliability of the analyses."

◆ **They assessed the breadth of data they wanted to analyze.** What data was important? What information would they need that was currently only on paper? They brought their performance evaluation data, competency assessments and succession planning information into the electronic fold. This gave IFC "a far richer pool of HR data to analyze than our current HR transactional system alone."

◆ **They supplemented their HR data with operational data.** Once this information was fully integrated, a more complete picture emerged which could inform strategy.

Continued on next page

Continued from previous page

With this critical blending of data, Fucello was able to analyze the productivity and efficiency of the organization's regional department by the number of deals closed per investment officer. "It's a much better measure of staffing efficiency than traditional HR ratios of professional to administrative staff."

IFC has used analytics to delve into troubling turnover issues with its investment staff and ensure that the ratio of nationalities among its work force is consistent with shareholder expectations. It used its data to tackle a key strategic need to deploy more experienced and senior staff, currently Washington-based, closer to its clients in Latin America, Middle East, Africa and Asia.

Before implementation, the organization "spent as much as 80 percent of our time gathering and manipulating the data and only 20 percent actually analyzing it. Work force analytics reverses that ratio ... We've been able to shift from the 'how many ...' questions to more strategic 'why' questions that uncover causes and solutions."

Joe Fucello, "The Emerging Mandate For Workforce Analytics," HR.com

The Quiz

1. Metrics aren't typically used by HR departments for the simple reason that HR's contribution can't be measured in numbers.

   ❏ True ❏ False

2. Cost-per-hire is still the most effective measure of recruiting effectiveness.

   ❏ True ❏ False

3. The best metrics for your organization won't necessarily be best for your key competitor.

   ❏ True ❏ False

4. The information you gather is useless if you don't follow through with concrete action.

   ❏ True ❏ False

Answer key: 1. F; 2. F; 3. T; 4. T.

What are you accountable for?

Essential skills for HR professionals

Whether your company has dozens or thousands of employees, your compliance administration activities and strategic responsibilities demand a comprehensive—and diverse—set of skills and competencies.

WHAT you need to know

> Remember that first and foremost, your role is that of a business advisor whose specialized knowledge is in human resources. You're accountable for the success of the business in the same manner as any other business leader in any other functional area, whether it is operations, finance or sales.

Accordingly, you need to consider every problem that faces the business as one that HR has the potential to help solve. Are sales declining, for example? That's not just a problem for sales, that's HR's problem as well. What can HR do to make a difference in declining sales? Ask yourself these kinds of questions:

- ◆ Is there open headcount in sales?
- ◆ Are positions not being filled rapidly enough?
- ◆ What is the voluntary and involuntary turnover among the sales staff?
- ◆ What is the compensation plan; are salespeople incented and compensated appropriately?
- ◆ How about sales management?
- ◆ Is additional training required?
- ◆ Is more effective performance management necessary?
- ◆ Are poor sales performers demoralizing the remainder of the sales force?

Your list could go on and on. And for each problem that the business confronts, whether it's "people" related or not, your job as an HR professional is to evaluate what HR can do to assist in solving that problem. Don't make the mistake, as many professionals do, of tuning out when the business talk turns to other functional areas. This is when you should be listening, learning and problem solving.

If you approach each business problem that your organization faces with the attitude that HR is accountable for participating in the solution, you will develop the strategic expertise necessary to be seen as a valued partner.

DON'T miss this

What competencies should you cultivate?

HR professionals have a key role in compliance adherence, human capital development and achieving the company's strategic goals. Performing these functions requires commitment and skill, and sometimes some of the competencies need to be developed so that HR can perform their roles effectively. Competencies that will help you perform well in HR's dual roles of compliance administration and strategic operations include the following:

Analytical skills. Handling and accurately interpreting large amounts of information. Separating symptoms from causes. Understanding the "big picture."

Business knowledge. Knowing your industry, the customers' business needs, and your company's business. Understanding and using the language of business. Understanding how HR can add value to the company's business.

Bottom-line mindset. Seeking profit improvements. Using business cases to sell the financial value of HR services, systems and programs. Using the language of business to demonstrate how HR's human capital management activities contribute to the company's success. Focusing on solving business problems to help achieve the company's strategic objectives.

Coaching ability. Mentoring employees and managers to help them develop as individuals, as well as to help drive change needed to accomplish business goals. Sharing knowledge and understanding with others. Demonstrating how to perform tasks when necessary. Using positive reinforcement to encourage and motivate individuals.

Communication skills. Being a good listener and asking questions. Repositioning problems into opportunities. Speaking and writing with clarity and persuasiveness. Preparing and presenting an effective business case. Developing relationships throughout the company to get to know the business and understand how the corporate culture works. Explaining to employees, line managers, top managers and boards of directors how HR initiatives, compensation structures, performance management, policies and other factors are aligned with the company's strategic objectives.

Confidence. Making tough decisions after evaluating a situation. Being willing to make mistakes, and when mistakes are made, learning from them and moving on. Doing the research and business analysis to reinforce intentions.

Courage. Using tact, diplomacy and determination to say and do what needs to be said and done. Refusing to be a yes-man or yes-woman, but instead, developing logical business cases to illustrate problem-solving initiatives. Facing problems head-on. Taking responsibility for mistakes. Keeping employees, line managers and top managers informed of the truth.

Creative thinking skills. Considering all feasible alternatives for any situation. Taking original and innovative approaches in developing initiatives or solving problems. Looking beyond the obvious or traditional methods in search of new ways to develop or administer programs, to communicate with employees, to streamline workflow, to increase productivity and to solve business problems.

Customer focus. Talking with employees and managers and getting to know how their departments function. Asking them what their problems are, then asking how HR might be able to help them. Proactively developing ideas to help employees and managers maximize human capital and solve their problems.

Energy. Performing a significant amount of work over sustained periods of time. Maintaining broad intellectual interests and continually learning. Leading by example with enthusiasm and a positive attitude.

Flexibility. Thinking quickly. Adjusting quickly and effectively in an atmosphere of change. Being open-minded to alternatives. Allowing individuals to function within their own work style. Outsourcing HR functions when appropriate. Accepting that situations will not always go the way desired and moving on to the next issue. Adapting to working for companies in different industries and getting to know their businesses.

Integrity. Operating in an ethical and trustworthy manner. Maintaining confidentiality, telling the truth and being open to feedback. Keeping promises and being dependable. Providing accurate information. Complying with the law and ensuring that corporate representatives and managers comply with the law. Maintaining appropriate compliance administration activities.

Interpersonal competence. Understanding emotions and feelings and working with individuals using empathy as well as logic. Using politeness, tactfulness and diplomacy. Developing working relationships. Being open-minded in discussions and giving consideration to constructive criticism. Being punctual for meetings. Being respectful to others.

Leadership. Guiding by example in words and actions of honor, dependability, relationship-building, customer focus and business-driven activity. Stepping up to challenges. Being proactive in helping others to develop skills, in proposing business solutions to management and in anticipating the company's needs before problems or situations develop.

Objectivity. Remaining objective in decision-making activities, keeping the customer focus and business objectives in mind. Being balanced and emotionally in control. Maintaining a business focus and resisting temptation toward biases.

Remaining calm and impartial in frustrating situations, emotionally charged situations, or when dealing with irrational individuals.

Ombudsmanship. Constantly communicating with employees and staying knowledgeable about their needs. Representing employee perspectives to management. Helping to solve problems and to align activities that motivate and develop employees while helping to meet company objectives.

Patience. Using good listening skills and not reacting too quickly when someone is emotionally charged. Waiting and allowing others to take the time they need to consider issues or complete tasks.

Planning. Effectively managing tasks and time to maximize personal productivity. Helping employees and managers to improve workflow. Developing HR initiatives and anticipating problems, costs and other factors that will affect the success of the initiative. Looking at the "big picture" and projecting both short- and long-term activities and results, and communicating that information to management.

Political astuteness. Staying aware of internal power dynamics, including any remote locations. Recognizing and dealing effectively with hidden agendas. Understanding the informal as well as the formal organizational structure. Staying in tune with the corporate culture.

Pragmatism. Taking a leadership role in finding practical approaches to solving problems and developing ideas. Helping articulate and refine customers' vision and strategic direction. Using common sense and logic rather than emotion or bias.

Proactive attitude. Anticipating future needs, changes and problems. Taking an active role in initiating activities to address issues that affect human capital and business objectives.

Resourcefulness. Getting the maximum benefit from less-than-perfect situations. Doing a lot with a little. Finding ways to solve problems and create initiatives within the available resources.

Teamwork. Leading and motivating teams in working toward objectives. Participating as a team member who contributes ideas and provides constructive feedback. Building a teamwork atmosphere within the corporate culture. Unifying the HR team about their individual roles, the company's strategic objectives and how they can contribute to helping the business. Focusing on "we" rather than "I." Building consensus through communication and persuasion.

Technology-friendliness. Approaching computers, software, database management, the Internet and other technology as friends to HR, rather than enemies. Embracing the possible benefits in workflow, productivity, safety/ergonomics, customer service, product quality and other improvements that technology may bring in solving business problems and meeting corporate strategic objectives. Using technology as a tool for success, rather than viewing it as a threat to HR.

Vision. Conceiving ideas for enhancing human capital and for improving business operations. Envisioning the company's potential and communicating concepts to top management. Imagining possible futures, setting goals and developing business cases for activities to help maximize the company's potential. Understanding the problems that line managers of each functional area face, then helping the managers to achieve their vision (and helping them develop a vision if they don't have one).

Work ethic. Doing what needs to be done to get the job done well and on time. Going the "extra mile" for employees and management without being asked and without complaining. Working smart as well as working hard. Taking pride in the quality of work that plays a key role in the company's success.

These competencies comprise an important skill set that is invaluable to HR professionals.

DON'T miss this

Typically, however, all of these competencies are not fully developed in any one person, no matter how talented the individual. That's why it's important for you be aware of the skills you need to be an effective strategic HR professional, then to strive for continuous improvement personally and professionally in developing and maintaining these competencies.

Continually strengthening your skills will only enhance your abilities to help your company achieve its strategic objectives.

What is HR accountable for?

Remember—your goal is to work toward company objectives and to achieve positive business results. You have specialized talents for achieving your desired results. And your role in HR makes you accountable for many sensitive, vital functions that can have tremendous impact on both human capital and the success of the business. Use the following checklist to help you keep on track as you add value to achieving the company's objectives.

✓ Checklist

Accountabilities of a strategic HR professional

☐ Understanding the company's strategic objectives.
☐ Aligning HR's strategy to help meet the company's strategic objectives.
☐ Aligning HR resources and activities with the company's strategic objectives.
☐ Identifying the organization's business goals.
☐ Identifying the people capabilities HR needs to achieve those goals.
☐ Getting the right people in the right place for the right price at the right time.

- ☐ Asking HR's customers—top management, line managers, and employees—where they're headed and how HR can help them get there.
- ☐ Serving as an internal expert and advisor on both technical employment regulations and general management concepts.
- ☐ Proactively developing HR strategic plans to solve current business problems and anticipate and avoid future problems.
- ☐ Formulating practical business cases showing return on investment (ROI) for HR initiatives.
- ☐ Getting top management buy-in for HR strategic business cases.
- ☐ Understanding the corporate culture.
- ☐ Leading the way as a change agent for organizational change and improvements.
- ☐ Communicating business objectives and strategic goals to employees whose daily efforts will ultimately lead to success and encouraging productive feedback.
- ☐ Developing strategic influence.
- ☐ Implementing strategic plans and coordinating the efforts of everyone involved.
- ☐ Increasing employee productivity and corporate revenue.
- ☐ Reducing costs.
- ☐ Using metrics to provide measurable results on how HR is positively impacting the company's bottom line.
- ☐ Keeping the lid on consistently increasing HR budgets.
- ☐ Unifying everyone in HR to support and execute HR strategic plans.
- ☐ Outsourcing HR functions when appropriate to budgets and strategic objectives.
- ☐ Developing your business background and skills and understanding basic business terminology.
- ☐ Functioning as a businessperson whose specialty is HR.
- ☐ Serving as an ombudsman of the employees to top management.
- ☐ Operating as an honest, ethical and dependable professional.

Tools for aligning strategy with company objectives

As the previous list shows—and as has been discussed throughout this book—one of the primary responsibilities of an HR professional is to align HR strategy and resources with the organization's strategic objectives. To help clarify and summarize what this means, consider the actions many companies take to align their strategies.

According to a 2003 report, "Forging Strategic Business Alignment: Preliminary Findings," from The Conference Board, most companies use two basic managerial approaches to aligning strategy to corporate goals:

1. **"Hard-wired" approaches** emphasize controlling and coordinating work tasks and employees. These approaches accomplish the mechanics of execution, but they can be impaired by inability to respond quickly to change in the business environment and lack of voluntary cooperation.

2. **"Soft-wired" approaches** emphasize organic methods of managing. These methods can energize managers and employees, but they often fail to provide the structures or systems that are needed to further alignment in a business.

Although most companies surveyed used one or the other approach, each of these approaches has strong disadvantages. Therefore, it appears that a combination of the hard- and soft-wired approaches would create a balanced framework for a flexible and more durable form of strategic alignment.

You may be able to use some of the tools that are used by survey respondents to help align your HR activities with your company's goals. Note that the study focused on aligning strategy to corporate goals overall, not just the role of HR in strategic alignment, but even so the list illustrates some basic approaches that are applicable to HR.

According to the study, alignment tools that companies have used to enable and sustain strategic alignment are as follows. They're ranked from most beneficial to least beneficial by the survey respondents, with the lowest ranked activity being rated beneficial by at least half of the respondents:

◆ Focus on fewer priorities.
◆ Replacing executives.

- Corporate communication plan.
- Leadership development.
- Incentives/variable pay.
- Governance process for investments.
- Team-based culture.
- Change current operating practices.
- Training in alignment.
- Reorganization.
- Use of a scorecard.
- Empowerment.
- Employee surveys.
- Performance contracts.
- Headquarters oversight and control.
- Creating employment brand.

It's important to note how many of these tools fall into traditional HR responsibilities: corporate communication, leadership development, incentives/variable pay, team-based culture, training, empowerment and employee surveys. Taken as a whole, the list demonstrates just how much strategic influence HR can have in an organization—if you understand the business and devote your efforts toward making it succeed.

Alignment is not a single short-term project. You should expect the company's focus to continue to evolve over time. Aligning the organization behind the company's strategic direction requires leadership commitment at all levels—including HR—to achieve corporate goals. Alignment is an ongoing process and requires communication throughout the organization.

Your time is now

Your time to shine as a business partner on your company's strategic team is now. HR plays a bigger role now more than ever before in aligning human capital management with a company's strategic direction. This is true in part because of several shifts in the general business climate:

- The employment situation in the U.S. is dynamic, as industries continue to consolidate through mergers, acquisitions and bankruptcies. Cost-conscious employers are trimming work forces, cutting back on training, scaling back on travel and examining other ways to minimize resources in efforts to boost profitability.

◆ Jobs are becoming more knowledge-intensive. Many jobs that were previously considered "unskilled" now require the use of computers and other technology. For some companies, that means retraining or providing new training for employees to get them up to speed.

◆ Businesses need to get more done with fewer employees. New technologies have paved the way for staffing reductions in large organizations. But fewer people means those that remain must be highly competent and reliable—and they must be developed and retained.

◆ The work force is more mobile. Employees typically no longer expect job security in exchange for their loyalty. As a result, people realize they need to continually expand their range of skills and talents so they can change jobs as needed or desired.

◆ Employees have greater expectations for their work-life balance. Workers expect to "have a life" and not live for their jobs. Telecommuting, flexible schedules and a host of family-oriented benefits are needed to retain talent and maximize human capital.

DON'T miss this

If you're questioned about whether HR really can impact your company's success, cite the Malcolm Baldrige National Quality Award. It's regarded by many business leaders as the top award for organizational performance, and Baldrige winners consistently have outperformed the S&P 500. The award's criteria includes: human resources, leadership, strategic planning, customer and market focus, information and analysis, process management and business results. Clearly, HR can play a key role in these areas and thus has tremendous value to a company's profitability and reputation.

As you increase your knowledge and insight as a strategic thinker and businessperson, you'll increasingly be in a position to participate in developing the company's overall strategic vision so that you can ensure top management includes the human capital implications of the strategic plan.

??The Quiz

1. Which of the following is not an essential skill for HR professionals?
   a. Analytical skill.
   b. Business knowledge.
   c. Communication skills.
   d. Stenography skills.
   e. Integrity.
   f. Pragmatic approach.

2. Which of the following is not a responsibility for which HR professionals are accountable in a strategic operation?
   a. Understanding company strategic objectives.
   b. Aligning HR strategy with company strategic objectives.
   c. Increasing employee productivity and corporate revenue.
   d. Using metrics to provide measurable results.
   e. Functioning as a businessperson whose specialty is HR.
   f. Cleaning the cafeteria.

3. Strategic alignment is a short-term project that usually shows results within a few months.   ❏ True   ❏ False

Answer key: 1. d; 2. f; 3. F.

Index